Best of
F. B. Meyer

Christian Focus Publications

F. B. Meyer (1847-1929), an English Baptist
pastor, was a popular convention speaker in
Britain and America. He wrote many books which
are still widely read today. This book is a selec-
tion from these writings.

© Christian Focus Publications
ISBN 1-85792-108-9

Published by
Christian Focus Publications Ltd
Geanies House, Fearn, Ross-shire,
IV20 1TW, Scotland, Great Britain.

Printed and bound in Great Britain by
Cox & Wyman Ltd, Reading, Berkshire

Cover design by Donna Macleod

Contents

Sources of chapters

A small amount of editing has been done to some of the chapters.
(1) He Emptied Himself: *Commentary on Philippians*; (2) The
Name of Names: *Commentary on Philippians*; (3) Gethsemane:
The Way into the Holiest (an exposition of Hebrews); (4) The Fiery
Ordeal of Temptation: *The Call and Challenge of the Unseen*; (5)
'Ye Shall Be Holy': *Tried by Fire (an exposition of 1 Peter)*; (6)
The Victory of Calvary: *The Call and Challenge of the Unseen*; (7)
'Filled with the Holy Ghost': *Elijah and the Secret of his Power*;
(8) A Fisher of Men: *Peter, Fisherman, Disciple, Apostle*; (9) The
Sin of David's Life: *David, Shepherd, Psalmist, King*; (10) Preparing
for Pisgah: *Moses, the Servant of God*; (11) The Divine
Summons: *Abraham, or the Obedience of Faith*; (12) Arrest and
Defeat: *Joshua and the Land of Promise*; (13) The Banquet: *The
Shepherd Psalm*; (14) The Secret of Guidance: *Tracts*; (15) Burdens,
and What to do with Them: *Tracts*; (16) The Stewardship of
Money: *Tracts*; (17) Our Bible Reading: *Tracts*; (18) 'In a Strait,
Betwixt Two': *Paul, a Servant of Jesus Christ*; (19) 'How Large
Letters': *Paul, a Servant of Jesus Christ*.

1

He Emptied Himself

'Let this mind be in you, which was also in Christ Jesus: Who, being in the form of God, thought it not robbery to be equal with God: But made Himself of no reputation, and took upon Him the form of a servant, and was made in the likeness of men: And being found in fashion as a man, He humbled Himself, and became obedient unto death, even the death of the cross (Philippians 2:5-8).

In the whole range of Scripture, this paragraph stands in almost unapproachable and unexampled majesty. There is no passage where the extremes of our Saviour's majesty and humility are brought into such abrupt connection. Guided by the Spirit of God, the Apostle opens the golden compasses of his imagination and faith, and places the one point upon the supernal Throne of the eternal God, and the other upon the Cross of shame where Jesus died, and he shows us the great steps by which Jesus approached always nearer and nearer to human sin and need; that, having embraced us in our low estate, He might carry us back with Himself to the very bosom of God, and that by identifying Himself with our sin and sorrow He might ultimately identify us with the glory which He had with the Father before the world was. And this wonderful description of His descent to our shame and sorrow is here cited by the Apostle, that it might be a living impulse and inspiration to ourselves, not to look upon our own things, not to hold them with a tight grasp, but to be willing to stoop for others to shame, sorrow, and spitting; fulfilling God's purpose of mercy to the world, even as Jesus Christ, who became the instrument and organ through which God's redemptive purpose wrought. 'Let this mind be in you.' Think these thoughts. Never look exclusively upon your own interests, never count anything of your own worthy to stand in the way, but always be prepared to the last point to deny yourself, that the redemptive purpose of God may flow through the channel of your life to those that sorely need His blessed help. It is a wonderful thing that, day by day, in our poor measure, we may repeat the purpose and the work of Jesus Christ our Emmanuel.

No rhetoric or metaphor of ours can add to the splendour of these words, but in the simplest possible way we will stand on these seven successive slabs of chrysolite.

(1) He was in the Form of God

The Greek word translated 'form' means a great deal more than the external appearance; it stands for the essence of God's nature, so that we may say that Jesus Christ possessed the essence of the Divine quality and nature from all eternity. This exactly agrees with other words of Scripture, as when we are told, He is '*the image of the invisible God*'. Again, '*Being the effulgence of His glory*, i.e. He was the outshining beam of the Father's glory; 'and the *very image of His substance*, i.e. He corresponded to the Divine Nature, as a seal to the die. Again, '*The Word was with God, and the Word was God*'. '*All things were made by Him*.' And then, as we overhear that marvellous communion between the Son and the Father in John 17, we notice His reference to the glory He had with the Father before the worlds were made, and with which He asks the Father to glorify Him in His human nature again. All these deep words prove that whatever God was in the uncreated eternity of the past - the infinite, the incomprehensible, the all-holy, and the all-blessed - that was Jesus Christ, who was absolutely one with Him, as spirit and soul are one in the organisation of our nature.

(2) There was no robbery when He claimed equality with God

Indeed, as the RV puts it, it was *not a thing to be grasped*, because He was so sure of it. It was conceded to Him universally; He counted it no robbery; He thought it detracted nothing from the Father's infinite glory when He stood on an equality with Him; and it is remarkable to notice how in the four courts of earthly life He prosecuted His claim. There are four courts for us all.

In the court of His intimates. On the highway to Caesarea Philippi, He asked His disciples whom men took Him to be; and Peter cried, 'Thou art the Christ, the Son of the Living God'. This could not have meant that the Lord Jesus was the Son as we are sons. That would have been a meaningless response. There was something more than that. And Jesus took it to be more, because He said, 'Flesh and blood hath not revealed it unto thee, but My Father which is in heaven'. In those words He took to Himself the prerogative of equality with God. You remember how He said afterwards: 'Ye believe in God' - give Me the same faith, 'believe also in Me'. He thought it not robbery to receive the faith that man gives to God. He said significantly: 'My Father and I' - '*We* will come and make our abode with him'. He thought it not robbery to enter the human soul and to share its occupancy with the Father.

With His intimates He always spoke of Himself as One with the Father, in an incomprehensible, mysterious, but essential oneness.

So also in the court of public opinion. He said, 'I and My Father are One', with an emphasis that made the Jews catch up stones to cast at Him, because, being a man, He claimed to be God. And He also told them that all men were to honour the Son even as they honour the Father. He thought it not robbing God to accept the honour men gave to Him.

So also in the court of justice. We know how the priests challenged Him, and asked Him to declare His essential nature, and said, 'Art Thou the Son of the living God'? - using the word *son* in the sense the Jews always did use it, as intimating essential Deity; and He said, 'Thou sayest that I am: and hereafter ye shall see the Son of man coming in the glory of God' - for He did not think it robbery to share God's prerogative and place.

Finally, in the court of death. When death came, and He hung upon that cross of agony, He did not for a moment retract all that He had said, but opened the gate to the dying thief, and assured him that he would be that day with Him in Paradise - for He did not think it robbing God to assume the right of opening the gates of forgiveness and life.

All through His earthly life He insisted upon it that He was God's equal, God's fellow, and that He was One with the Father.

(3) He emptied Himself

This was evidently by His free will and choice. He emptied Himself *of His glory*. As Moses veiled the glory that irradiated from His Person. We are told they need no sun in heaven, because His Presence is sun. What an effulgence of light must have streamed from Jesus, the Second Person of the Holy Trinity, in those uncreated ages! But when He stepped down to earth He veiled it - the Word became flesh and tabernacled among us - the Shekinah nature was shrouded, so that it was not able to penetrate, save on the Mount of Transfiguration, when, for a moment, the voluntary act by which Christ hid His intrinsic splendour was laid aside, and it welled out in cascades and torrents of blinding light.

But probably we are specially here taught that He emptied Himself *of the use of His divine attributes*. This is a profound truth which it is necessary to understand if you would read rightly the lesson of our Saviour's life. Men have been accustomed to think that the miracles of Jesus Christ were wrought by the putting forth of His intrinsic and original power as God: that when He hushed the storm, and the waves crouched like whelps to His feet - that when He raised the dead, and Lazarus sheeted with grave-clothes came forth - that when He touched the sight of the blind, and gave eyeballs to those that had been born without their optics - that all this was done by the forthputting of His own original, uncreated, and divine power; whereas a truer understanding of His nature, specially as disclosed in the Gospel by St John, shows that He did nothing of Himself, but what He saw the Father doing; that the words He spoke were not His own words, but as He heard God speaking He spoke; that the works He did were not his own, but the Father's who sent Him, for when they said on one occasion 'Show us the Father', He replied, 'He that hath seen Me hath seen the Father; the words I speak to you I speak not from Myself, but the Father that dwelleth in Me, He doeth His works'. His human life was one of faith, even as ours

9

should be: 'As the living Father hath sent Me, and I live by the Father, even so he that eateth Me shall live by Me'. Frequently He paralleled our experience with His own; and no doubt the story of the Vine in which He depicts our dependence upon Himself, had long been in His thought as an emblem of His own dependence upon the Father. He chose to live like this. He voluntarily laid aside the exercise of His omnipotence, that He might receive power from God; absolutely and voluntarily forewent the use of attributes that lay all around Him, like tools within the reach of the skilled mechanic, that He might live a truly human life, weeping our tears, and receiving the plenitude of His Father's power.

(4) He took upon Him the form of a Servant

The infinite God, with whom He was One, desired to achieve certain purposes in our world; and the blessed Christ, the Second Person in the Trinity, undertook to be the medium and vehicle through which the Father might express Himself: and just as the words that issue from our mouth are impressed with our intelligence - the liquid air around us yielding itself to the movements of the larynx, so that what is in our mind is communicated and conveyed to others as they listen - so Jesus Christ became the Word of God, impressed with the thought, mind, and intention of God, so that the Father was able, through the yielded nature of the Son, to do, say, and be everything He desired. Christ was the perfect expression of the Being of Him whom no man hath seen, or can see.

It is so absurd, therefore, to divorce Jesus from the Father. Preachers have made an awful mistake when they have spoken of the Atonement as though Jesus intervened to appease the Father, to satisfy something in God that needed satisfaction before He could love. On the contrary, the whole Bible substantiates the belief that God was in Christ; and that what Christ did, God did through Him, and that the death on the cross was the act of the entire Deity. What wonder, then, that the Father said, 'Behold My Servant whom I have chosen, Mine elect, in whom My soul is well pleased. I will put My Spirit upon Him, and He shall show judgment to the Gentiles'.

(5) He was made in the likeness of men

He must know what the experiences of a human body are, what childhood and boyhood, and what it is to pass through the various stages of manhood. It was needful that He should be as perfectly united with man as He was perfectly united with God, so that He might be made a merciful and faithful High Priest, to make intercession for our sins; for all these reasons He did not abhor the Virgin's womb, but was made man. Let us not fear too much the mystery and burden of human life. Our Lord and Master has gone this way before us, and has left a track behind, as they who traverse the Australian bush break twigs or branches along their route to serve as a guide to those who follow. It is good to be born, that we may have a share in the nature He has worn.

(6) He died

He need not have died, because He was sinless; and death was only the result of sin. Adam sinned, and so died; Jesus did not sin, and therefore needed not to pass through death's portal. From the Mount of Transfiguration, He might, had He chosen, have stepped back into heaven, as Adam might have been caught back to God, if he had not eaten of the forbidden fruit. Had our first parents not yielded to temptation, our race would still have peopled the world, and would have passed away - as, at the Second Advent, those will, who are alive and remain - suddenly changed, not seeing death, and their mortality swallowed up of life. From the Mount of Transfiguration Jesus Christ could have stepped into heaven, His body passing in a moment, in the twinkling of an eye, through its supreme transfiguration. But, had this been the case, He would never have made the reparation due to the holy law which man had broken. And therefore, with calm deliberation, and with full knowledge of all that awaited Him, He came down the mountainside, and yielded Himself to death. He laid down His life at the cross, and bowed His meek head beneath death's sceptre. He had power to lay down His life, as a voluntary gift and sacrifice for our race; and He used it. Though Lord of all, He became obedient to the last dread exaction of human penalty: and, through death, destroyed him that had the power of death.

(7) He chose the most degrading and painful form of death

There were several methods of death - by decapitation, by the stoppage of the heart's action, or by drinking poison. The death of the cross was the death of the slave, the most shameful and ignominious. Cicero said that it was far, not only from the bodies but the imagination of Romans. Therefore, since this death was the most shameful through the exposure of the person, the most degrading, the most painful known to man, the Saviour chose it. He could not have gone any lower.

One has sometimes imagined how He might have died - in the home of Bethany, with the window open towards

Jerusalem, Mary wiping the death-dew from His brow, and Martha waiting on His every need, whilst Lazarus gave Him a brother's help. But this could not be the Lord's choice, in view of the fact that He must taste death for every man, and be made a curse, and be able to put His everlasting arms beneath those of His followers, who have died the most excruciating and shameful deaths.

We must be willing to lay aside our ambition and glory, our thrones of comfort, respect and power, if by doing so we may be the better able to succour others. We must be willing to take the form of servants, to wash one another's feet, to submit even to shame and spitting, to misunderstanding and opprobrium, if we shall thereby help to lift the world nearer God. There is no other way of sitting with Jesus on His throne, no other method by which we may assist Him, however feebly, in his work of saving others. There are plenty among us like the two brethren who would sit right and left in the Kingdom, who will never be able to attain thereto because they will not pay the price of drinking His cup and being baptised with His baptism. They will not take the low seat, or stoop to the obscure and unnoticed tasks: they love the honour that comes from human applause, and the notoriety which accrues from conspicuous notices in the daily press. God help and forgive us for yielding to these insidious temptations, and give us the Spirit of our Lord, that the same mind may be in us as in Him. Kepler, when he first turned his telescope to resolve the nebulae, said, 'I am thinking over again the first thoughts of God'; but surely it is given to us to think still earlier thoughts than those of Creation, even those which were in the heart of the Lamb who was slain in the Divine Purpose before the worlds was framed.

2

The Name of Names

'Wherefore God also hath highly exalted Him, and given Him a name which is above every name: That at the name of Jesus every knee should bow, of things in heaven, and things in earth, and things under the earth; And that every tongue should confess that Jesus Christ is Lord, to the glory of God the Father' (Philippians 2:9-11).

This is the other side of the subject we last considered. Then, we contemplated the descent; now, the ascent: the one, His humiliation; the other, the glory to which God hath exalted Him. We ought to put this passage alongside of Ephesians 1:15-23, where the Apostle asserts that God displayed in the person of Jesus His mightiest power, when He raised Him from the dead, and set Him at His own right hand, far above all principality and power, might, and dominion, and every name that is named, not only in this world, but in that which is to come. Indeed all through the New Testament the Father's agency in the exaltation of His Son is distinctly accentuated; and we are constantly reminded of the contrast between the action of men, who with wicked hands crucified and slew Him, and the action of God, who raised Him from the dead.

There are two interpretations, which are suggested by the Authorised and Revised Versions. We are told in the RV that God highly exalted Him, and gave Him *the* name which is above every name - the emphasis on the definite *the*; and if we should accept this rendering, it would convey the meaning that the infinite God gave to Jesus, His perfected Servant, His own incommunicable name of Jehovah. The name which is above every name is manifestly the name of Jehovah, which the Jews held to be so sacred that they never mentioned it, never even wrote it. It is important for us to realise that in Jesus Christ there blend at this moment the perfected beauty of the Man and the excelling glory of Jehovah - the glory which He had with the Father before the world was made. That is so deep and blessed a truth that we may be quite prepared to admit it is included in the meaning here, for our Saviour is God.

But after looking carefully into the matter from every point of view, it seems better to come back to the conclusion suggested by the Authorised Version - that the name of Jesus, which was given to Him in His birth, has been recognised as the highest type of being in the whole universe, and that this name, or more especially the nature for which the name stands, is the loftiest and supreme type of character, which is highly exalted above all other characters and types of being. His is the conquering name; the name which shall become victorious; the name which is destined to supremacy - the name of Jesus. It was given to Him first by the angel Gabriel, when in his annunciation to the mother he said, 'Thou shalt conceive and bring forth a son, and shalt call his name Jesus'. And when Joseph was considering whether or not he should put away Mary, then espoused to him but not yet married, the angel of God, in a dream, told him to take to himself Mary his wife, because she would bear a son, to whom they must give the name Jesus. This name of Jesus was borne by our Lord throughout His earthly life, and often used by His apostles after His ascension, as the spell and talisman of victory, when they wrought miracles in His name. It is repeatedly referred to in the Epistles, and especially in that to the Hebrews, and evidently stands for the highest type of being. In the whole realm of existence this is the name which is above every name, that at the name of Jesus, the Saviour, every knee should bow in heaven, in earth, and in Hades.

(1) We obtain instruction

We are familiar with the phrase, 'Survival of the fittest'; by which we understand that amid the shocks and collisions of creation certain types of creature-life, stronger than others, broad-shouldered and powerful, have pushed their way to the front, and have crushed out the weaker. Amid the strife chronicled by history, certain races of mankind inevitably go down, whilst others forge their way to the front and hold positions of supremacy. Similarly, in the life of the world around us, where everything is being searched and tested to the uttermost by the ordeal of time, probation and trial, certain types of character are constantly being thrust downward, or hurled against the wall in the impetuous rush, whilst others come easily to the front. Thus, perpetually, different types of ideal and character are acknowledged as supreme.

As we look around us, in the great arena of life, we are often disposed to imagine that the type of character represented by power, by the giant's grip, by sinew and muscle, is the supreme and victorious one. At other times we are disposed to think that the type of the scientist and philosopher, the man of wise thought and penetrating investigation, is the elect, the ideal type. Again we are disposed to think that the man of wealth, who by his ingenuity has succeeded in accumulating a fortune or in building up a great business, exhibits the ideal type. Thus amid the cross-lights of this world we are greatly perplexed; for when we turn to the life of Jesus Christ, the sweet, gentle, self-denying, and forgiving life, which appeared to be unable to hold its own against the antagonism and malice of men, we are apt to conclude that that type at least is too tender, too gentle, too retiring and unobtrusive to become the dominant type. Yes, we exclaim, the race is to the strong, the sceptre for the wise, the throne for the man of wealth; but the cross is for the character that lives to love and forgive, and save.

It is good, therefore, to come into the sanctuary of God, to leave behind us our newspapers and novels, the standards of the market-place and the forum, and to submit our minds beneath the influence of this word which lets in eternity upon time, which allows the light that plays around the throne of God to strike in upon us; and, as we see things for one brief hour, not from the standpoint of our fellows, but of the angels - not judging by the standards of this world, but by those of the other world into which we so soon shall come - we shall find that the dominant type of character which is to endure, to last supreme when all other types of character, which men have worshipped and idolised, have passed away as the mists of winter before the summer, is the name and nature of Jesus Christ, the Saviour and Redeemer of men.

This is what God hath chosen. Here is the survival of the fittest. Here is the supreme conception of character. This, this is what eternity enthrones. This is what dominates angels and demons. The nature that stoops, loves, forgives, saves; *this* is the ideal type. God hath given Him a name above every name - Jesus, Saviour.

(2) We get great encouragement

It is of infinite importance to know what God loves best. We are destined to live with Him for ever, to see Him face to face, and be for ever in His presence. It is of the highest importance, therefore, to us to know what is His chosen ideal, that we may begin to shape ourselves by it, that we may emulate it, that we may ourselves seek to be endued by it, so that hereafter we may be taken to the bosom of God as His chosen friends and children. If we desire to know a man we must converse with him, enter his study, handle and look at his books, and gaze round the walls at the pictures he has chosen to adorn them.

If we know a man's ideal, we know him. If we can only get God's ideal, we may know Him. Where can we find it? In creation? No, not His deepest. In proverb and prophecy? No, not His deepest. In angels excelling in strength? No, not His deepest. In the perfection of moral character? That is nearer, but it is not His deepest. The name that is dearest to God is *Jesus*; and the character which is dearest to God is that which bears, forgives, and loves even to death, that it may save. That which God sets His heart upon for evermore is redemptive love, which He glorifies, raising it to the highest place that heaven affords.

'Ah, we will not fear Thee more, our God! We have stood under the thunder-peal hurtling through the air, and trembled; we have beheld the lightning-flash revealing our sin and making us cry for shelter; we have watched Thy march through history, and there have been traces of blood and tears behind on Thy track; and as we look out into the eternal future our hearts stand still. We are but leaves in the great forest of existence; bursting bubbles upon the mighty ocean of being; but when we come to see that Thine ideal is in the Divine Man who died for us, we fear Thee no more, but approach with the confidence of a little child; for if Thou dost love the Man Christ Jesus, and we love Him too, we can meet Thee in the Cross with its dying agony.' It is a great encouragement to know that God's ideal is the Man who died.

Our God seems sometimes to come near us and say: 'There is never a soul that stoops, stripping itself that it may wash the feet of another; there is never a soul that sheds tears over the ruin of those it loves, as Jesus did on the Mount of Olives over Jerusalem; there is never a soul that pours out its life-blood even unto death; there is never a soul that denies itself to the uttermost, that is not dear to Me. I notice it, though the great world passes by unwitting and careless; I bend over those who tread in the earthly pathway trodden by My Son, My well beloved; and though the midnight darkness may gather over the head, extorting the cry, 'My God, my God, why hast Thou forsaken?' I do not forget, I cannot forsake; and presently, when the earth has passed away like the shadow of the cloud upon the hills, I will gather such, and bear them upward, taking them to My bosom, and enthroning them right and left of My Son. He that drinks the cup which Jesus drank of, and is baptised with the baptism with which he was baptised, though forgotten, ignored, crushed and trampled underfoot by men, shall sit beside the Son of Man in His kingdom.'

Oh, let us take heart, as we think of God's ideal; let us be encouraged, for now we know what God is, and that ultimately He will vindicate our work of faith, and labour of love, and patience of hope.

(3) We get exhortation

The name of Jesus is, then, dear to God. What then? Let it be your plea, for it is said that whosoever believeth in that Name shall receive remission of sins. Convicted sinner, longing to have a clue to the maze, go at this moment into the presence of the great God and plead the name of Jesus. Let your one cry be founded upon what He was, and is; and just so soon as you utter that name, in the spirit of the name, God accepts, forgives, and saves.

Live in that name - in the temper and character of Jesus - day by day; let His gospel imbue and colour your character; let the imitation of the life of Jesus be the one object of your ambition. There is no other clue to life amid the misery and sorrow of the world. Sometimes it seems hard to remember that children laugh, that the sun shines yet, that the crocuses and snowdrops are preparing to break through the clods of winter. We live oppressed beneath the infinite anguish and agony of the world; it is so dark, so terrible with its sin and sorrow, with its overcrowding and drink and passion; and there is one's own broken life, and all the mystery and perplexity of God's dealings. We can find no clue to it except to follow the ideal of Christ, living to save; every day by patient and tender forbearance making someone happier; lifting the burden from some shoulder, sending a rift of light into some darkened heart. There is no other clue for the difficulty and perplexity of life.

Sunday School teacher, never let the lesson pass without allowing the Name of Jesus Christ to mingle with your words, like the breath of flowers in the summer air. Preacher, see to it that that Name rings through your utterances, your first word and your last. It is the only spell and talisman of victory; it is the one name that will overcome the power of the devil in temptation, and before which the evil spirits that beset us in our hours of weakness and depression give back. It is the watchword for those who approach the portals of eternity; the talisman of victory in the hour of death.

As soon as you utter the name of Jesus, you arrest the Divine ear. Therefore in every prayer, before you break out into adoration, praise, confession or entreaty, speak in the ear of God that name. Remember that Jesus said: Whatsoever ye ask the Father in My Name, in My Nature, according to the ideal of My life, He will give you. Let the name of Jesus winnow out of your prayers everything proud, selfish and vindictive; let them be poured like liquid and gleaming metal into that precious mould.

Reverence that name. 'In the name of Jesus every knee shall bow.' Let us never utter it without the prefix *Lord*. Let Him be always the *Lord* Jesus. If God speaks His name with marked emphasis, we must treat it with devout reverence. I greatly shrink from too great familiarity with the precious name of our Lord. A man has to be very near the Great Brother who can call him familiarly by His name.

'And every tongue confess.' Let us confess that He is Lord. God the Father has made Him His ideal type; make Him your ideal type. God has just put the sceptre into His hand, do you put the sceptre into His hand also. God has enthroned Him, do you enthrone Him too, and today look up and say: 'Henceforth, Blessed Jesus, Thou shalt be Lord and King; Lord of my life, King of my mind and heart; my Lord and my God'.

And remember that that is the one hope of the future. That name of Jesus, whispered first by Gabriel to Mary and to Joseph, spread through a comparatively small circle of

His immediate followers, but at Pentecost the Holy Ghost caught it up, and spoke it in thunder; and ever since it has been spreading through the world and through the universe, and we are yet to see the time when the loftiest angels shall bow beneath it, when all men shall own it, and the very demons acknowledge it. 'Jesus I know, and Paul I know', was the sad confession of a fallen spirit centuries ago.

This name of our Lord - the last name spoken on earth, the first name uttered in heaven - the name that comprehends grace, the name that spells glory, for He has gone to prepare a place for us. We have passed the shortest day; yonder is the spring and summer of the morning land, and we anticipate the time when we shall sit with Him; bearing that name with Him; and perhaps going forth to all parts of the universe to tell of it, to kindle hearts and lives with it, to unfold, as only redeemed men can, the full meaning and significance of the name Jesus.

3

Gethsemane

*'Who in the days of his flesh, when he had offered up prayers
and supplications with strong crying and tears unto Him
that was able to save Him from death, and was heard in that
He feared; though he were a Son, yet learned He obedience
by the things which He suffered' (Hebrews 4:7, 8).*

Eight ancient olive trees still mark the site of Gethsemane;
not improbably they witnessed that memorable and mysterious scene referred to here. And what a scene was that! It
had stood alone in unique and unapproachable wonder, had
it not been followed by fifteen hours of even greater mystery.

The strongest words in the Greek language are used to
tell of the keen anguish through which the Saviour passed
within those garden walls. 'He *began* to be sorrowful'; as
if in all His past experiences He had never known what
sorrow was! 'He was sore amazed'; as if His mind were
almost dazed and overwhelmed. 'He was very heavy', His
spirit stooped beneath the weight of His sorrows, as afterwards His body stooped beneath the weight of His cross; or
the word may mean that He was so distracted with sorrow,
as to be almost beside Himself. And the Lord Himself
could not have found a stronger word than He used when
He said, 'My soul is exceeding sorrowful, even unto death.'

But the evangelist Luke gives us the most convincing
proof of His anguish when he tells us that His sweat, like
great beads of blood, fell upon the ground, touched by the
slight frost, and in the cold night air. The finishing touch

is given in these words which tell of His 'strong crying and tears'.

The things which He suffered

What were they? *They were not those of the Substitute*. The tenor of Scripture goes to show that the work of Substitution was really wrought out upon the cross. There, the robe of our completed righteousness was woven from the top throughout. It was on the *tree* that He bare our sins in His own body. It was by His *blood* that He brought us nigh to God. It was by the *death* of God's Son that we have been reconciled to God; and the repeated references of Scripture, and especially of this epistle, to sacrifice, indicate that in the act of dying, *that* was done which magnifies the law and makes it honourable, and removes every obstacle that had otherwise prevented the love of God from following out its purposes of mercy.

We shall never fully understand here how the Lord Jesus made reconciliation for the sins of the world, or how that which He bore could be an equivalent for the penalty due from a sinful race. We have no standard of comparison; we have no line long enough to let us down into the depths of that unexplored mystery; but we may thankfully accept it as a fact stated on the page of Scripture perpetually, that he did that which put away the curse, atoned for human guilt, and was more than equivalent to all those sufferings which a race of sinful men must otherwise have borne. The mystery defies our language, but it is apprehended by faith; and as she stands upon her highest pinnacles, love discerns the meaning of the death of Christ by a spiritual instinct, though as yet she has not perfectly learnt the language in which to express her conceptions of the mysteries that

24

circle around the cross. It may be that in thousands of unselfish actions, she is acquiring the terms in which some day she will be able to understand and explain all.

But all that we need insist on here and now is that the sufferings of the garden are not to be included in the act of Substitution, though as we shall see they were closely associated with it. Gethsemane was not the altar, but the way to it.

Our Lord's suffering in Gethsemane could hardly arise from the fear of His approaching physical sufferings. Such a supposition seems wholly inconsistent with the heroic fortitude, the majestic silence, the calm ascendancy over suffering with which He bore Himself till He breathed out His spirit, and which drew from a hardened and worldly Roman expressions of respect.

Besides, if the mere prospect of scourging and crucifixion drew from our Lord these strong crying and tears and bloody sweat, He surely would stand on a lower level than that to which multitudes of His followers attained through faith in Him. Old men like Polycarp, tender maidens like Blandina, timid boys like Attalus, have contemplated beforehand with unruffled composure, and have endured with unshrinking fortitude deaths far more awful, more prolonged, more agonizing. Degraded criminals have climbed the scaffold without a tremor or a sob; and surely the most exalted faith ought to bear itself as bravely as the most brutal indifference in the presence of the solemnities of death and eternity. It has been truly said that there is no passion in the mind of man, however weak, which cannot master the fear of death; and it is therefore impossible to suppose that the fear of physical suffering and disgrace could have so shaken our Saviour's spirit.

But He anticipated the sufferings that He was to endure as the propitiation for sin. He knew that He was about to be brought into the closest association with the sin which was devastating human happiness and grieving the Divine nature. He knew, since He had so identified Himself with our fallen race, that, in a very deep and wonderful way, He was to be made sin and to bear our curse and shame, cast out by man, and apparently forsaken by God. He knew, as we shall never know, the exceeding sinfulness and horror of sin; and what it was to be the meeting-place where the iniquities of our race should converge, to become the scapegoat charged with guilt not His own, to bear away the sins of the world. All this was beyond measure terrible to one so holy and sensitive as He.

He had long foreseen it. He was the Lamb slain from before the foundation of the world. Each time a lamb was slain by a conscience-stricken sinner, or a scapegoat let go into the wilderness, or a pigeon dipped into flowing water encrimsoned by the blood of its mate, He had been reminded of what was to be. He knew before His incarnation where in the forest the seedling was growing to a sapling from the wood of which His cross would be made. He even nourished it with His rain and sun. Often during His public ministry, He was evidently looking beyond the events that were transpiring around Him to that supreme event, which He called 'His hour'. And as it came nearer, His human soul was overwhelmed at the prospect of having to sustain the weight of a world's sin. His human nature did not shrink from death as death; but from the death which He was to die as the propitiation for our sins, and not for ours only, but for those of the whole world.

Six months before His death He had set his face to go

to Jerusalem, with such a look of anguish upon it as to fill the hearts of His disciples with consternation. When the questions of the Greeks reminded Him that He must shortly fall into the ground and die, His soul became so troubled that He cried, 'Father, save me from this hour!' And now, with strong cryings and tears, He made supplication to His Father, asking that if it were possible, the cup might pass from Him. In this His human soul spoke. As to His Divinely-wrought purpose of redemption, there was no vacillation or hesitation. But, as man, He asked whether there might not be another way of accomplishing the redemption on which He had set His heart.

But there was no other way. The Father's will, which He had come down from heaven to do, pointed along the rugged, flinty road that climbed Calvary, and passed over it and down to the grave. And at once He accepted His destiny, and with the words, 'If this cup may not pass from Me, except I drink it, Thy will be done', He stepped forth on the flints that were to cut those blessed feet, drawing from them streams of blood.

His Strong Crying and Tears

Our Lord betook Himself to that resource which is within the reach of all, and which is peculiarly precious to those who are suffering and tempted - He prayed. His heart was overwhelmed within Him; and He poured out all His anguish into His Father's ears, with strong crying and tears. Let us note the characteristics of that prayer; that we too may be able to pass through our dark hours, when they come.

It was *secret prayer*. Leaving the majority of His disciples at the garden gate, He took with Him the three who had

27

stood beside Jairus' dead child, and had beheld the radiance that steeped Him in His transfiguration. They alone might see Him tread the winepress: but even they were left at a stone's cast, whilst He went forward alone into the deeper shadow. We are told that they became overpowered with sleep; so that no mortal ear heard the whole burden of that marvellous prayer, some fitful snatches of which are reserved in the Gospels.

It was *humble* prayer. The evangelist Luke says that He knelt. Another says that He fell on his face. Being formed in fashion as a man, He humbled Himself and became obedient to death, even the death of the cross. And it may be that even then He began to recite that marvellous Psalm, which was so much on His lips during those last hours, saying, 'I am a worm, and no man; a reproach of men and despised of the people'.

It was *filial* prayer. Matthew describes our Lord as saying, 'Oh my Father'; and Mark tells us that He used the endearing term which was often spoken by the prattling lips of little Jewish children, *Abba*. For the most part, He probably spoke Greek; but Aramaic was the language of His childhood, the language of the dear home in Nazareth. In the hour of mortal agony, the mind ever reverts to the associations of its first awakening. The Saviour, therefore, appearing to feel that the more stately Greek did not sufficiently express the deep yearnings of His heart, substituted for it the more tender language of earlier years. Not 'Father' only, but 'Abba, Father!'

It was *earnest* prayer. 'He prayed more earnestly', and one proof of this appears in this repetition of the same words. It was as if His nature were too oppressed to be able to express itself in a variety of phrase; such as might

28

indicate a certain leisure and liberty of thought. One strong current of anguish running at its highest could only strike one monotone of grief, like the note of the storm or the flood. Back, and back again, came the words, *cup... pass... will... Father*. And the sweat of the blood, pressed from His forehead, as the red juice of the grape beneath the heavy foot of the peasant, witnessed to the intensity of His soul.

It was *submissive* prayer. Matthew and Mark quote this sentence, 'Nevertheless, not what I will, but what Thou wilt.' Luke quotes this, 'Father, if Thou be willing, remove this cup from me; nevertheless, not my will, but thine be done.'

Jesus was the Father's Fellow - co-equal in his Divine nature; but for the purpose of redemption it was needful that He should temporarily divest Himself of the use of the attributes of His deity, and live a truly human life. As man, He carefully marked each symptom of His Father's will, from the day when it prompted Him to linger behind His parents in the temple; and He always instantly fulfilled His behests. 'I came down from heaven,' He said, 'not to do mine own will, but the will of Him that sent Me.' This was the yoke He bore, and in *taking* it, He found rest unto His soul. Whatever was the danger or difficulty into which such obedience might carry Him, He ever followed the beacon-cloud of the Divine will; sure that the manna of daily strength would fall, and that the deep sweet waters of peace would follow where it led the way. That way now seemed to lead through the heart of a fiery furnace. There was no alternative than to follow; and He elected to do so, nay, was glad, even then, with a joy that the cold waters of death could not extinguish. At the same time, he learnt what obedience meant, and gave an example of it, that shone out with unequalled majesty, purity and beauty, unparalleled in the annals of the universe. As man, our Lord then learnt how much was meant by that word *obedience*. 'He learned obedience.' And now He asks that we should obey Him, as He obeyed God. 'Unto them that obey Him.'

Sometimes the path of the Christian's obedience becomes very difficult. It climbs upward; the gradient is continually steeper; the foothold ever more difficult; and, as the evening comes, the nimble climber of the morning creeps slowly forward on hands and knees. The day is never greater than the strength; but as the strength grows by use, the demands upon it are greater and the hours longer. At last a moment may come, when we are called for God's sake to leave some dear circle; to risk the loss of name and fame; to relinquish the cherished ambition of a life; to incur obloquy, suffering and death; to drink the bitter cup; to enter the brooding cloud; to climb the smoking mount. Ah! then we too learn what obedience means; and have no resource but in strong cryings and tears.

In such hours pour out thy heart in audible cries. Plentifully mingle the name 'Father' with thine entreaties. Fear not to repeat the same words. Look not to man, he cannot understand thee; but to Him who is nearer to thee than thy dearest. So shalt thou get calmer and quieter, until thou rest in His will; as a child, worn out by a tempest of passion, sobs itself to sleep on its mother's breast.

The Answer

'He was heard for His godly fear.' His holy reverence and devotion to His Father's will made it impossible that His prayers should be unanswered; although, as it so often happens, the answer came in another way than His fears had suggested. The cup was not taken away, but the answer came. It came in the mission of the angel that stood beside Him. It came in the calm serenity with which He met the brutal crowd, that soon filled that quiet garden with their coarse voices and trampling feet. It came in His triumph and the grave. It came in His being perfected as mediator, to become unto them that obey Him the author of eternal salvation, and a High Priest for ever after the order of Melchisedec.

Prayers prompted by love and in harmony with godly fear are never lost. We may ask for things which it would be unwise and unkind of God to grant; but in that case, His goodness shows itself rather in the refusal than the assent. And yet the prayer is heard and answered. Strength is instilled into the fainting heart. The faithful and merciful High Priest does for us what the angel essayed to do for Him; but how much better, since He has learnt so much of the art of comfort in the school of suffering! And out of it the way finally emerges into life, though we have left the right hand and foot in the grave behind us. We also discover that we have learnt the art of becoming channels of eternal salvation to those around us. Ever since Jesus suffered there, Gethsemane has been threaded by the King's high-way that passes through it to the New Jerusalem. And in its precincts God has kept many of His children, to learn obedience by the things that they suffer, and to learn the Divine art of comforting others as they themselves have been comforted by God.

There are comparatively few to whom Jesus does not say, at some time in their lives, 'Come and watch with Me'. He takes us with Him into the darksome shadows of the winepress, though there are recesses of shade, at a stone's cast, where He must go alone. Let us not misuse the precious hours in the heavy slumbers of insensibility. There are lessons to be learnt there which can be acquired nowhere else; but if we heed not His summons to watch with Him, it may be that He will close the precious opportunity by bidding us sleep on and take our rest; because the allotted term has passed, and the hour of a new epoch has struck. If we fail to use for prayer and preparation the sacred hour, that comes laden with opportunities for either; if we sleep instead of watching with our Lord; what hope have we of being able to play a noble part, when the flashing lights, and the trampling feet announce the traitor's advent? Squander the moments of preparation, and you may have to rue their loss through all the coming years!

4

The Fiery Ordeal of Temptation

'Christ was tempted in all points as we are, yet without sin' (Hebrews 4:15; see also 2:9, 10).

What is God doing at this moment? He may be creating new worlds; may be working up into new and beautiful shapes what we should account as waste products; or may be preparing to unveil the new heavens and the new earth. But there is one thing of which we may be sure: He is bringing many sons unto glory! In order to help these to the uttermost, the Son of God was tempted in all points as we are, yet without sin. It was real temptation, for He suffered being tempted; but being perfected through the terrible ordeal, He has become the Author of eternal salvation to all who obey Him. Let us learn His talisman of victory!

This bringing of many sons unto glory is a long and difficult process, for three reasons:

(1) It is necessary that we should be created as free agents, able to say 'No' as well as 'Yes'.

(2) We have to choose between the material world, which is so present and very attractive to our senses, and the eternal, spiritual and unseen. But the choice is inevitable if we are to really know things. We can only know a thing by contrast with its opposite.

(3) There is a realm of evil spirits constantly regarding us with envious hatred and bent on seducing us from the paths of goodness and obedience. They are adept at their art.

If it be asked why we are placed in circumstances so perilous, so trying, the answer, so far as we can formulate it, is that we are being tested with a view to the great ministries awaiting us in the next life. We are to be priests and kings! There are vast spaces in the universe that may have to be evangelised or ruled or influenced for righteousness. It may be that important spheres of ministry are needing those to fill them who have learnt the secret of victory over materialism on the one hand and over the power of Satan on the other. We know that there was war in heaven before Satan and his angels were cast down to earth, and there may be another, and yet another. Therefore earth may be the school, the training-ground, the testing-place for the servants and soldiers of the hereafter. This thought need not be in conflict with the ideals of rest and worship which we are wont to associate with the future life. Eternity will give opportunities for all! But, if it became Him of whom and through whom are all things to make the Captain of their salvation perfect through the suffering of temptation, it stands to reason that His comrades and soldiers must pass through the same, that they may become more than conquerors and, having overcome, may sit with Him on His throne, as He overcame and is set down with His Father on His throne.

The First Temptation on record is that of our First Parents in Eden
It is a masterpiece of psychology! The experience of all after-time has added nothing to this marvellous analysis.

(1) Temptation is more formidable when we are alone! Solitude is full of peril, unless it is full of Christ!

(2) Some outward object, or some fancy of the mind,

attracts our attention. It may be an apple, a face, a gratification, the lure of popularity, or money. The longer we look at it the stronger the fascination grows. Some birds are mesmerised by the fixed gaze of their foe at the foot of the tree. The longer we gaze at something forbidden, the stronger its mesmeric power. Whilst we continue to look, the tempter covers the walls of imagery with more definite and attractive colours, and his ideals imperiously demand realisation in act. Our only hope is to tear ourselves away from those basilisk eyes; to hasten from the haunted chamber; to escape, as Joseph did in the house of Potiphar.

(3) If we linger, many thoughts will gather to ply us - all of them suggested by the tempter, who speaks through the voice of our own soul. These suggestions will question the love and wisdom which have forbidden. 'Perhaps we have placed an exaggerated interpretation on our limitations and prohibitions. Are they not rather arbitrary? Would it not be good to know evil just once, that it might be avoided ever after? Besides, is it not necessary to know evil in order to realise good? Perhaps it would be better to satisfy the inner craving for satisfaction by one single act; then the hungry pack of wolves would at least be silenced! After all, is it not probable that if one were to know the forbidden thing it would be so much easier to warn others?' Such are the reasonings in which the tempted shelter themselves, not realising that the only certain way of knowing evil is not by committing, but by resisting it.

(4) Finally, we take the forbidden step, eat the forbidden fruit; the garment of light which veiled our nakedness drops off; the tempter runs laughing down the forest glade; a shadow falls on the sunshine, and a cold blast whistles in the air. Our conscience curses us, and we die, i.e. we cease

35

to correspond to our proper environments, which are God, purity and obedience. Eve ought to have dropped that apple like a burning coal, and hurried from the spot; but, no; she lingered, ate, and gave to her husband; so sin entered into the world; and sin opened the door to pain, travail, sorrow, the loss of purity, the loss of God's holy fellowship in the cool of the day, the fading of the garden, and the reign of death and the grave.

The Temptation of our Lord

(1) It came after the descent of the Spirit as a dove. We may always expect deep experience of the tempter to follow close on the highest moments of spiritual exaltation. Where you have mountains you must look for valleys!

(2) He was led of the Spirit to be tempted; clearly, then, temptation is not a sin. A holy nature might go through hell itself, assailed by clouds of demons, and come out on the farther side untainted. So long as the waves of evil break on the outward bulwarks of the spirit they are innocuous. Jesus was tempted in all points as we are, yet without sin.

(3) The sword of the Spirit and the shield, against which the darts of evil fall blunted to the ground, are the words of the ever-blessed God, and the upward glances of a steadfast faith. Remember how Jesus said, 'It is written'; 'it is written again'. He is also the Pioneer and Perfection of faith!

(4) Each temptation which He overcame seemed to give Him power in the very sphere in which it had sought His overthrow.

He was tempted to use His power to satisfy His own hunger; but, having refused to use it selfishly, He was able to feed five thousand; and four thousand men, besides women and children.

He was tempted to cast Himself from the wing of the temple to the dizzy depth below, in order to attract attention to Himself; but having refused, He was able to descend into Hades, and then ascend to the Father's throne; to lay down His life and take it again for a world of sinners.

He was tempted to adopt Satan's method of gaining adherents by pandering to their passions; but He refused, and adopted the opposite policy of falling into the ground to die, of treading the winepress alone, of insisting that it is not by yielding to passion, but by self-denial, self-sacrifice and the Cross that salvation is alone to be obtained. Therefore, a great multitude, which no man can number, have washed their robes and made them white in His blood, and stand before the throne.

Having, therefore, met temptation in the arena, and mastered it in its threefold spheres - the lust of the flesh, the lust of the eyes, and the pride of life - Jesus is able to succour them that are being tempted; and if they should fail He is able to understand, because He has gone every step of the way Himself and is well acquainted with its perils. He can easily trace the lost sheep on the mountains, because He has marked every pitfall and the lair of every enemy. He has looked over the cliff-brink to the bottom, where those who have missed the track 'in the cloudy and dark day' may be lying; and when He has found them He brings them home on His shoulder rejoicing.

Our Own Temptations
We all have to pass through the wilderness of temptation, the stones of which blister our feet, and the air is like a sirocco breath in our faces.

(1) All God's sons are tempted. As we have seen, we

only know light by darkness, sweet by bitter, health by disease, good by evil resisted and overcome.

> ' "Oh, where is thy sea?" the fishes said,
> As they swam through the crystal waters blue!'

They had never been out of it, and so were in ignorance of that which had always been their element.

(2) The pressure of temptation is strictly limited. When Satan approached God with regard to Job, he was on two occasions restricted to a fixed barrier, beyond which he might not go. In the case of Peter also, when he obtained permission to approach him, he could only go so far as to sift him as wheat; he might rid him of chaff, but not hurt anything essential. Remember also that glorious announcement: 'There hath no temptation taken you but such as man can bear: but God is faithful, who will not suffer you to be tempted above that ye are able; but will with the temptation also make a way of escape, that ye may be able to endure it' (1 Corinthians 10:13).

(3) As you live near God the temptation gets deeper down in your nature. You are aware of it in subtler forms and disguises. It attacks motives rather than the outward habits and actions.

One summer afternoon, when I came down to the Auditorium at Northfield, USA, I found Mr Moody and his brother on the platform, and between them a young apple tree, just digged up and brought from the neighbouring orchard. There were about a thousand people in the audience. When I reached the platform the following dialogue took place.

Mr Moody to his brother: 'What have you here?'

'An apple tree,' was the reply.

'Was it always an apple tree?'

'Oh no, it was a forest sapling, but we have inserted an apple graft.'

Mr Moody to me: 'What does that make you think of?'

'You and I were forest saplings,' said I, 'with no hope of bearing fruit, but the Jesus-nature has been grafted into us by the Holy Spirit.'

To his brother: 'Does the forest sapling give you trouble?'

'Why, yes,' said the gardener. 'It is always sending out shoots under the graft, which drain off the sap.'

'What do you do with them?'

'We pinch them off with our finger and thumb; but they are always coming out lower down the tree.'

Then he turned to me and asked if there was anything like it in the spiritual life, to which I replied: 'It is a parable of our experience. The old self-life is always sending out its shoots, and we can have no mercy on them; but if we deal with the more superficial sins on the surface of our life, as we get older we realise their deeper appeals, and to the end of life shall be more and more aware of their sinister power. The quick sensitiveness of age must not be ignored or overlooked. It may be as strong a shoot in the old forest sapling as the manifestations of passion in earlier life. Old men, for instance, may be jealous of young ones, and quick to take offence if there are symptoms of their being put aside'.

(4) Temptation is not in itself sin, but we cannot say, as our Saviour could, 'The Prince of this world cometh, and hath nothing in me'. We cannot appropriate those last words. We know that all the inner gunpowder magazines are not emptied. Therefore it is just as well, after a severe

time of testing, as the demons leave us, to ask ourselves if there has been some subtle response in the depths of our nature it may be forgiven. We must not risk the loss of ship or cargo because the combustion is so slow and so deep in the hold.

(5) In the hour of temptation affirm your union with your all-victorious and exalted Saviour! Stand in His victory! You are part of His mystical Body; take your rightful position! God has set Him at His own right hand in the heavenlies; be sure to come down on your foe from the heights of the throne. It is always easier to fight down from the mountain slope than up from the lowland valleys. You can be more than a conqueror through Him that loved you; but abide in Him.

(6) Always ask the Saviour to hold the door on the inside. Satan will burst it open against *your* feeble strength; but when Jesus stands within all hell will be foiled. Though ten thousand demons are at you, in your patience possess your soul!

(7) One other point is of immense importance. Be sure to claim the opposite grace from Christ. The fact that an attack is being made at a certain position in your fortifications proves that you are weakest there. When therefore the tempter advances to the attack, and you are aware of his strategy, take occasion to claim an accession of Christ's counter-balancing strength. When tempted to quick temper, 'Thy patience, Lord!' To harsh judgment, 'Thy gentleness, Lord!' To impurity, 'Thy purity, Lord!'

By all hell's hosts withstood,
We all hell's hosts o'erthrow;
And conquering still by Jesus' blood,
We on to victory go.

Sometimes temptation will come upon us in the hatred and opposition of man, and we shall be strongly tempted to use force against force, strength against strength, and to employ weapons of flesh and blood. This is not the best. The raging foe is best encountered by the quiet faith and courage which enable a man to go boldly forward, not yielding, not daunted, not striking back. Hand the conflict over to the Captain of your salvation. It is for you simply to stand in the evil day, and having done all, to stand.

Love the truth more than all, and go on in the mighty power of God, as good soldiers of Jesus Christ; in nothing daunted by your adversaries, but witnessing a good confession, whether man will bear or forbear. 'Greater is He who is in you than he that is in the world.'

It may be that this earth on which we find ourselves is the Marathon or the Waterloo of the universe. We are as villagers who were born on the site and are implicated in the issues of the war. We are not merely spectators but soldiers, and whether in single combat or in the advance of the whole line, it is for us to play a noble part. Full often in the history of war the achievements of a single soldier have changed the menace of defeat into the shout of victory. Think of David's conflict with Goliath; of the three that held the bridge in the brave days of old; and of the Guards at Waterloo! From their high seats the overcomers, who in their mortal life fought in the great conflict for the victory of righteousness and truth, are watching us. Are they disappointed at our handling of the matter? Are we worthy to call ourselves of their lineage, or to be named in the same category? Fight worthily of them, whether in private secret combat, or in the line of advance, that you may not be ashamed at the grand review!

Fight first against the wicked spirits that antagonise your own inner life. Repeat the exploits of David's mighties: of Benaiah, who slew a lion in a pit in time of snow; of the three who broke through the Philistines' lines and drew water from Bethlehem's well for their king; of Amasai and his host, the least of whom was equal to a hundred. Every lonely victory gained in your closet and in your most secret sacred hour is hastening the victory of the entire Church. Listen! Are not those the notes of the advancing conquering host? Are not the armies of Heaven already thronging around the Victor on His white horse?

It is high time to awake out of sleep! The perfecting of God's purpose is at hand! The return of the Jews to Palestine; the budding of the fig tree; the bankruptcy of politicians and statesmen; the threatened overthrow of European civilisation; the rise of Bolshevism; the new grouping of the nations for war, notwithstanding the appeals of the League of Nations; the awful havoc of Spiritism; the waning of love; all these are signs that we stand at the junction of two ages. The one is dying in the sky, tinting it with the sunset; the other is breaking in the East, and the cirrus cloudlets are beginning to burn. Let us then put off the works of darkness and put on the armour of light, now in the time of this mortal life, that when He shall come in His glorious majesty to receive the kingdom of the world, we may rise to the life immortal, through Him who liveth and reigneth with the Father and the Holy Spirit, one God, blessed for evermore!

Fight the good fight with all thy might,
Christ is thy strength, and Christ thy right;
Lay hold on life, and it shall be
Thy joy and crown eternally.

5

'Ye Shall Be Holy'

*'Wherefore girding up the loins of your mind, be sober and set
your hope perfectly on the grace that is to be brought unto you
at the revelation of Jesus Christ; as children of obedience, not
fashioning yourselves according to your former lusts in the
time of your ignorance: but like as He which called you is holy,
be ye yourselves also holy in all manner of living; because it is
written, Ye shall be holy; for I am holy. And if ye call on Him
as Father, who without respect of persons judgeth according to
each man's work, pass the time of your sojourning in fear'
(1 Peter 1:13-17 RV).*

The 'wherefore' with which this paragraph opens gathers
up the premises of the preceding verses, and uses them as
a massive platform of solid masonry on which to erect the
battery of appeal to which the Apostle now addresses
himself. Because our destiny is what it is; because Jesus
Christ is what He is; because our salvation has been the
theme of prophets, apostles, martyrs, angels; *therefore*...

And the *aim of his appeal is Holiness*. 'Be ye yourselves also holy in all manner of living.' The cry for
HOLINESS rings through the Bible. It is the keynote of
Leviticus, from which this quotation is made (cf. verse 16
with Leviticus 11:44; 19:2; 20:7 and 26, etc.); and it is
equally the supreme demand of the New Testament. In
point of fact, all the wondrous machinery of redemption,
from the distant choice of eternity to the descent of the
Holy Spirit on the Day of Pentecost, has had this for its

purpose, that we, who have been the subjects of the grace of the Persons of the Eternal Trinity, should resemble them in the holiness which is the perpetual burden of heaven's rapturous minstrelsy - that song which was heard by the evangelical prophet Isaiah from the Temple courts, in the year that King Uzziah died; but which was still unfinished when the beloved Apostle John detected it amid the break of the Aegean Sea around the lone island of his banishment; and which will never cease, world without end: 'Holy, holy, holy, is the Lord God the Almighty' (Isaiah 6:3; Revelation 4:8).

Holiness is the property of God alone. It is the totality of the Divine attributes; the sum of the Eternal and Infinite Being of Godhead; the essence of Deity; the chord made by the harmonious blending of Divine qualities; the beam woven from the many colours of Divine perfections; the expression in a single term of all that goes to make up the moral nature of the great Spirit whom we call GOD. It is underived in its source; unlimited in its measure; insupportable in its naked and unveiled splendour by the eye of any creature which He has made. 'Who is like unto Thee, O Lord, glorious in holiness, fearful in praises, doing wonders?' (Exodus 15:11). No tongue then shall dare to challenge God's right to declare Himself as the Holy One of Israel, or to say in the words before us, 'I am holy'.

Such holiness is evidently possible to us. See, the holy God has 'called' us to it (1 Peter 1:15). 'God hath not called us to uncleanness, but to holiness' (1 Thessalonians 4:7). He 'hath called us with an holy calling' (2 Timothy 1:9). All partakers of the heavenly calling are called holy brethren (Hebrews 3:1). But God would not summon us to heights we could not scale, or to tasks we could not

44

perform. His CALL involves two facts - first, that his holiness is within our reach; secondly, that He is prepared to supply all that is necessary to effect in us that to which He calls us. God is pledged to make us holy; or He will expose Himself to the mockery of his foes. But we need not fear for Him. He counted the cost before He issued his proclamation; and He is well able to finish that of which He laid the foundation in the great depths of Calvary (Luke 14:29, 30).

Nor is such holiness for saints and apostles alone; or only for the special golden days which visit most lives - days of feast and song and transfiguration. The Divine ideal is more comprehensive far. 'Holy in all manner of living' (verse 16). Zechariah foretold the time when the inscription on the high priest's mitre should be written even on the bells of the horses: 'Holiness to the Lord'. And it is God's will that that motto should be engraved on house bells, and office bells, and shop bells; on dinner bells and factory bells; so that in every department of our lives there may be sweet music made to life's great Lord. Holiness at every turn, and in every incident of our daily walk, like the golden tinkle which betrayed each movement of Israel's high priest (Exodus 28:33-35; Zechariah 14:20, 21).

There is only one way of becoming holy, as God is: and it is the obvious one of opening the entire being to the all-pervading presence of the Holy One. None of us can acquire holiness apart from God. It dwells in God alone. Holiness is only possible as the soul's possession of God; nay, better still, as God's possession of the soul. It never can be inherent, or possessed apart from the Divine fulness, any more than a river can flow on if it is cut off from its fountain head. We are holy up to the measure in which we are God-possessed. The least holy man is he who shuts God up to the strictest confinement, and to the narrowest limits of his inner being; partitioning Him off from daily life by heavy curtains of neglect and unbelief. He is holier who more carefully denies self, and who seeks a large measure of Divine indwelling. The holiest is the man who yields himself most completely to be influenced, swayed, possessed, inspired by that Spirit who longs to make us to the fullest extent partakers of the Divine nature.

Wouldst thou be holier? There is but one way. Thou must have more of God in thee. Holiness is the beauty of the Lord God of hosts. Thou canst not separate the one from the other. To have *it* thou must have *Him*. Nor will it be hard to obtain either; for He longs to enter into thy being. Thy longing is the faint response of thy heart to His call. The power that works within is matched by the grace which can do for us exceeding abundantly above all that we ask or think. Man never desired so much of God as God desired of man. God's holiness has revealed itself in a human form in the person of Jesus Christ our Lord; and so it is as able as it is eager to enter human lives through that blessed Spirit who is pre-eminently the channel and medium by which we are filled up unto all the fulness of God. Ask thy heavenly Father for this Spirit. He is more eager to give Him than a father to give food to his hungry child. And, having asked, dare to believe that thou hast received, and 'go in this thy might' (Judges 6:14).

And this holiness will reveal itself in many ways.

(1) There will be the Pilgrim Attitude and Temper
Eastern fashions suggest the figure of *the girt loins*. There the loose and flowing robes suit well the deliberate move-

ments which the climate begets; but they would grievously hamper pilgrim, wrestler, or warrior. When the Israelites were momentarily expecting the summons for the Exodus, they stood with their loins girt around the tables on which the paschal lamb was smoking. Thus too did the prophet of fire gird himself for the swift courier-run before Ahab's chariot, from Carmel to Jezreel (1 Kings 18).

Our souls are clad with the flowing garments of various tastes, appetites, affections and propensities, which hang loosely around us, constantly catching in the things of the world, and hindering us in the Christian race. We must not let them stream as they will - or we do so at our peril. Absalom rued the day when his luxuriant tresses floated behind him in the breeze. We must 'gird up' the habits of our souls, and trim ourselves, so as to pass as quickly and easily as possible through the thorny jungle of the world.

Hold your spirit in a tight hand. Put a curb on appetite. Say 'No' to luxurious pleasure-seeking. Curtail your expenditure on yourself. Do not spread yourself too widely. Watch eye and lip, thought and wish, lest any break from the containing cords of self-control. 'Keep thy heart with all diligence.' Give Vanity Fair as little chance as possible, by passing swiftly and unostentatiously through.

Be sober! Sobriety is a great word. It is constantly inculcated in the New Testament on elders, deacons, women, aged men, young men and maidens. It means temperance, self-control, and a just estimate of one's self in the world. There are some who counterfeit it by assuming an austere and forbidding attitude, denouncing much that is innocent and natural, and looking severely on some who do not yield to their scruples. The truly sober man, on the other hand, moves freely through the world, strewn with beautiful and innocent things: using them without abuse, rejoicing in every good thing which the Lord God gives; but never allowing any of them to usurp too great an influence on his affections, or to tyrannise over his will.

When the heart is fully engaged with the Lord, His service, and love, and rewards and welcome home at last, it can afford to look undazzled on many a captivating spectacle, and to turn from many a fascinating cup. The holy heart, filled to brimming with the presence of God, is like a man who has been well banqueted, and who is therefore able to look calmly on the passionate heat with which starving men will fight with each other over offal.

Hope to the end. 'Set your hope perfectly' (RV). Go fearlessly as far as hope can go. Let her sit at her easel, painting her fairest pictures, or sing rapturously her most ecstatic lay: she cannot be disappointed. The 'grace which is to be brought unto us' when the veiling clouds are rent, and the Lord Jesus is revealed from heaven, will far surpass all her imaginings. Hope is the lamp of the soul, passed down from saint to saint, as in the old Greek race, but destined to be eclipsed in the light which is to break ere long upon our spirits - the day of perfected redemption, of glorified creation, of a perfected church. The Revised Version reminds us that that grace is being brought - it has started, and is already on its way.

(2) There will be the Obedience of Children (verse 14)
Once the children of disobedience, we have been born again, and become children of obedience - a fair mother with noble offspring. Such, at least, is the literal rendering of the Greek. And what a marvellous difference at once comes over the lives of those who have passed through this

change! They 'no longer fashion themselves according to the former lusts'.

Lust is natural inclination run wild, overleaping all restraint, and asserting its own imperious will. When we are yet in the darkness of nature, unillumined by the grace of God, these lusts fashion us. Beneath their touch we are moulded or *fashioned*, as clay by the potter's hand. Ignorant of the abominableness of sin, of its disastrous results, of its insidious growth, we yield to it until it becomes our tyrant and our ruin. Oh, the horror of the awaking, should we see the depths of this beetling precipice descending sheer beneath us to hell! When we no longer fashion ourselves according to the former lusts, but according to the will of God - that is *obedience*.

It is impossible to exaggerate the importance of this truth. Obedience is not holiness; holiness is the possession of the soul by God. But holiness always leads to obedience. And each time we obey, we receive into our natures a little more of the Divine nature. 'If ye shall indeed obey My voice, ye shall be a holy nation unto Me.' Do, then, whatever it is right to do. Forsake all which begins and ends with self. Be not satisfied with prayer and desire, but *DO*. And thus there will come over your face and life more likeness to the Father of your spirits; and you will be holy.

How few Christian people seem to realise that obedience in trifles, in all things, to the will and law of Jesus, is the indispensable condition of life and joy and power. The obedient soul is the holy soul, penetrated and filled by the presence of God, and all aglow with light and love. Dear reader, resolve from this moment to live up to the margin of your light. Let this be your motto: 'All that the Lord hath said will we do, and be obedient'. Israel said this and failed

49

utterly and shamefully; do you say it by the power of the Holy Spirit, and He shall make it gloriously possible.

(3) There will be a Reverent Anticipation of the Father's Award (verse 17)

God's children are to be judged, not at the great white throne, but at the judgment seat of Christ (2 Corinthians 5:10). That judgment will not decide our eternal destiny, because that has been settled before; but it will settle the rewards of our faithfulness or otherwise (Matthew 25:19; 1 Corinthians 3:14).

There is a sense in which *that judgment is already in process*, and we are ever standing before the judgment bar. 'The Father who *judgeth*.' The Divine verdict is being pronounced perpetually on our actions, and hourly is manifesting itself in light or shadow.

But it is a *Father's judgment*. We call on Him as Father. Notice this reciprocity of calling. He called us; we call Him; His address to us as children begets our address to Him as Father. We need not dread His scrutiny - it is tender. He pities us as a father pities his children, knowing our frame, allowing for our weaknesses, and bearing with us with an infinite patience.

But for all that *it is impartial*. 'Without respect of persons.' Many years before, this had been revealed to the Apostle from heaven in a memorable vision, which affected his whole after-ministry (Acts 10:35). Not according to profession, or appearance, or any self-constituted importance, but according to what we do, are we being judged.

The holy soul realises this; and a great awe falls upon it and overshadows it - an awe not born of the fear which hath torment, but of love. It passes the time of its sojourn-

50

ing in fear. Not the fear of evil consequences to itself, but the fear of grieving the Father; of bringing a shadow over His face; of missing any manifestation of His love and nearness to Himself, which may be granted to the obedient child. Love casts out fear; but it also begets it. There is nothing craven, or fretful, or depressing; but a tenderness of conscience which dreads the tiniest cloud on the inner sky, such as might overshadow for a single moment the clear shining of the Father's face. So the brief days of sojourning pass quickly on, and the vision of the Homeland beckons to us, and bids us mend our pace.

6

The Victory of Calvary

Paul left Athens in a very chastened mood. His address on Mars Hill had failed to produce the effect for which he had hoped. Two converts alone rewarded his efforts, and no church was formed there. He had argued, on the general grounds of Divine Creatorship and Providence, of human accountability and resurrection, of man as the offspring of God, and the absurdity of idolatry: but so far as the record of his address goes, there was no mention of the Cross. Was that the cause of his failure? Was it on his solitary walk along the isthmus between Athens and Corinth that he made up his mind to know nothing at Corinth but Christ crucified, and the Cross as God's powerhouse for those that believe? The careful reading of the early chapters of his first letter to the Church at Corinth will go far to confirm this suggestion.

Let us come to that Cross once more, remembering that it is the reflection in the waters of time of the dateless resolve of Eternity; for the Lamb was slain from the foundation of the world. Here is one of God's eternal facts translated into the language of today.

Let us imagine that we are strangers in Jerusalem, drawn from all parts of the Roman Empire to witness the rites of the Hebrew Passover, of which the fame has gone out into all the world. So crowded is the city that no hostel or caravanserai can give us room. We are obliged, therefore, to spend the brief warm night on the Mount of Olives, hard by the little villages of Bethphage and Bethany. With the first glint of the dawn, we arise and prepare ourselves for a day which shall be as our natal day, a day of days! We descend the mountain, leaving Gethsemane on the right, and cross the valley while the sun is low and climbing slowly above the horizon. Thus we find ourselves standing at the great closed gates of the city, in company with a group of peasants, who have brought their oranges, their figs, bananas, and the produce of their gardens, for sale in the bazaars. Presently the massive doors swing back. We enter and make our way at once to the magnificent stairway that leads to the Court of the Gentiles, beyond which we may not go. We pass across the vast tessellated floor to the eastern colonnade, with its matchless view of the hills of Moab towering to the right above the sullen waters of the Dead Sea. Before us is the Jordan Valley and the pasture lands beyond, whilst turning northwards we catch a distant glimpse of the great mountain ranges, which helped to make an heroic race, as the wars for freedom proved.

Above us are the Temple buildings, but thither we may not go, for 'the Beautiful Gate' at the head of the steps will admit none but Jews. We can, however, hear the exquisite music of the Hebrew choir, and one verse is translated for us which runs thus:

God is the Lord, who has shown us light;
Bind the sacrifice with cords even to the horns of the altar.

On reaching the foot of the great staircase, as we return, we are caught in a vast crowd of people, flowing in a tumultuous torrent in one direction; and presently find ourselves on the edge of a multitude that fills a spacious square from side to side. They are swaying to and fro under the influence of intense excitement, as waves swept by wild winds. This is the more remarkable as the day is still young. On the farther side of this piazza, immediately fronting us, is a magnificent building, under the portico of which two prominent figures are standing. The splendid dress of the one clearly indicates his rank and authority, whilst the man beside him is as evidently one of the people. These are obviously the centres of attraction to this vast, excited crowd.

Turning to a bystander, we ask him if he can explain the meaning of the extraordinary scene.

'Ah,' he replies, 'clearly you are strangers in the city, or you would not need to put that question. Yonder is the palace of the Roman Governor, and he is standing there. Those two soldiers behind him, with sheathed axes, are the lictors carrying the insignia of his rank. Beside him is a man called Jesus of Nazareth, whose name for the last three years has been on everyone's lips. He has confined himself mostly to the northern parts of this country, where He has carried on a great ministry of healing and preaching. Tens of thousands have assembled to hear Him, and this has aroused the envy of our religious leaders, who are determined to make away with Him. That dark-faced man yonder is the High Priest, Caiaphas, and I promise you that he will have his way, as a wild beast pulls down its quarry.'

'What charges are they bringing against Him?' we ask.

'There's the rub,' replies our informant. 'They have been trying to trump up a charge against Him for the last three hours. If bribes to false witnesses, and the ransacking of every deed and word capable of being twisted to serve an evil interpretation, could have done it, it would have been done. But neither money nor false swearing could make out a case that would hold water. In my opinion He is a white soul, and thousands more think the same. Only half an hour ago, on my way here, I was met by a man I used to know, and as he passed me he said in tones that chilled my heart, "I've betrayed innocent blood", and he ought to know, because he has been His intimate companion. They have eaten the same food, slept out under the same skies, and shared cloud and sunshine. If any one should know, he should. From the desperate look on his face, I expect that by this time he has committed suicide. But besides this, this Jesus has never been known to confess sin, though He is one of the humblest men that ever lived. With us Jews, the holiest of our race, men who claim to have seen the face of God, have been the first to confess that they were undone, the chief of sinners, and the least of saints. But though this Man has lived in God, none has ever heard Him sigh in penitence or utter a word of compunction. Besides this, He has been the means of lifting hundreds of debased men and women into pure and shining lives. Pure in heart Himself, He has made them pure! The publicans and sinners believe in Him, and they of all others can detect counterfeits.'

Is that so? Then since God is the Lord and He hath shown us light, bring *a white cord* and bind us to one of the horns of that altar of surrender and consecration. Here and now let us register ourselves among His followers. All the world beside is smitten with leprosy; but He can make us pure in heart and able to see God.

A bystander, who has overheard our conversation, says that he can add a further instance to prove that yonder prisoner is no ordinary man. He says: 'I was returning home late last night, from a friend's house, when I was attracted by a patrol of armed men, who were evidently set on a night arrest. I followed behind them, until at the entrance of a garden, known as 'the Garden of the Wine-press', I found that they were about to arrest this Jesus. But to my surprise, when He came out to meet them, it seemed as though they received a shock of power from His person which flung them backwards on the ground. When they recovered themselves, one of His followers, who clearly knew little about sword-exercise, made a stroke at one of the leaders of the band, and nearly severed his ear; whereat yon Man, whose wrists were tightly bound, asked liberty for His right hand, and reaching it out, touched and healed the ear, and gave His hand back to be bound.

'Now I said to myself: If He can do that, He is able to free Himself from this troop. Yet to my surprise, He allowed Himself to be led as a sheep to the slaughter. I had become so interested that I followed the band back to the High Priest's palace, and managed to get in with the crowd. There I witnessed the most astounding scene of all. As my friend here has told you, they sought all night to establish a charge against Him.

'Finally, when he saw the whole case breaking down, the High Priest arose and, amid the tense silence of the court, put their Prisoner on His oath, and asked if He were the Son of the ever-blessed God. His judges bent forward and hardly breathed as they awaited His reply. He had not spoken before, but being challenged thus, He stood erect, and with a light on His face that seemed the seal and endorsement of the Almighty, He said: "I am, and one day you shall see Me seated at the right hand of Power, and coming in the clouds of Heaven." That sealed His fate. They unanimously agreed that He should die; but, if you had known His character, as the purest and humblest of men, and if you had seen that light, you could not have doubted His assertion that He is God manifest in the flesh.'

Is that so? Is yonder Man really God in the likeness of human nature? Is He the mystic ladder that links God and man, the Mediator, the Daysman who can lay His hands upon us both? Then fetch *a golden cord* and bind us to the altar of fellowship and union with Him, that we may realise what all the rites and philosophies of pagan temples have failed to afford. God is the Lord and He has this day shown us light!

Here a woman who has been attentively listening, breaks in. 'May I speak?' Certainly! 'Ah!' she says, 'you men may talk about His goodness and deity, but there is more than that which accounts for the love which has poured out to welcome Him from every town and nearly every home in Galilee. He is full of selfless love. I remember that once I was staying at a mountain village, where the only son of his widowed mother had died and was being borne to his burial. At that moment *He* happened to come up, took in the situation at a glance, stopped the procession, made the bearers lower the bier, removed the cerecloth, took the hand of the young man, though it involved His ceremonial pollution, told him to arise as though He were awakening him from sleep, gave him back to his mother, and passed on without waiting for a word of thanks.

'He was always doing things like that; and didn't the people love Him! When He visited a town or village the children trooped around, sure of a smile. He never sent them away. I have seen a little boy nestling next to His heart, as He spoke to the people. Aye, He is one of the purest, gentlest, most loving of men, and always had a word

57

for those who were weary and heavy-laden.'

Again, we are arrested. Is not this what the world and we are waiting for? We seem to have been living in the Arctic Zone. Lover and friend can only wade a little distance with us into our 'river of sorrow'. The big selfish world rolls past us in its chariot, indifferent to our appeals for help. But is there love in the heart of that lone Man, which can change winter to summer, tears to smiles, and loneliness to fellowship? If so, thank God for showing us light and love on the face of the Son of Man. Fetch a *blue cord*, for blue is the colour of depth, of the azure sky, of the deep ocean, of the crevasse and the gentian, and bind us to the third horn of that altar of consecration.

But, finally, there is one other, who is eager to add his testimony. He says: 'I am a native of the lands on the farther side of the Jordan. It is a much wilder country than this; as you see, I have no pretence to education or the polite manners of the city. I learnt all I know from a marvellous man, who was the son of our wilder life. They called him the Forerunner; his name was John the Baptist. He was too straight for most of them, and they foully murdered him in his prison cell to please a wanton girl. I was standing with him, some three years ago, when yonder Man passed before us, and my master said, "There goes the Lamb of God, who will bear away the sin of the world". I asked him what he meant. He answered that he was not quite sure, but that he had an impression that He would do effectively what the sacrifices of our Temple did only in type. I know nothing more, but when I came by just now I saw the soldiers standing by three crosses, and I heard one of the High Priest's household say to another, "If our master gets his way, he will have Jesus of Nazareth on one of these crosses before many hours have passed". For my part, I believe that that man spoke the literal truth, and if it turns out to be so, you may be sure that He will bear away the sin and punishment, which no animal sacrifice could atone for.'

This is indeed new light on the approaching tragedy, which is infinitely more than a tragedy. We are witnessing a sacrifice, but clearly it is absolutely voluntary. All the people around us give the assurance that He could easily have left the country and hidden Himself. But apparently He deliberately put Himself within the reach of His implacable foes. One of His sayings is recorded to the effect that He came, not to be ministered to but to minister, and to give His life a ransom for many. Is that so? Is He bearing away my sin? By His stripes can I be healed? Is God in this wonderful Man reconciling the world to Himself, by a voluntary sacrifice? Then fetch *a crimson cord*, the emblem of blood, and bind us to that fourth remaining altar-horn. We need to be forgiven and to be forgiven righteously. If our Creator suffers for us, our redemption is certain. God is the Lord, and He has shown us light on the forgiveness of sin; and that crimson hue shall remind us of its cost.

While we have been talking thus, a murmur has been rising around us and spreading through the crowd. 'Not this man, but Barabbas!' We learn that the latter had raised an insurrection against the Roman Government, in which murder has played a part, and he was to be crucified with two confederates this very afternoon. Clearly the prediction of our last informant is likely to be realised, and presently Pilate gives sentence as is desired, releasing Barabbas and, after scourging Jesus, delivers Him to be crucified.

How he must have cringed as through the window

Barabbas heard his name shouted by ten thousand throats. His immediate conclusion was that he was going to be lynched, as soon as he emerged from the condemned cell. When the gaoler came down the corridor to lead him out, may he not have said: 'I suppose they are going to tear me limb from limb, before I reach the cross'. 'No, indeed,' would be the reply, 'lucky for you, your cross is wanted for another, and you are a free man.' 'A free man! What do you mean! Who is going to take my place?' 'Ah, there's the mystery of it! Jesus of Nazareth is to have your cross!' 'Jesus of Nazareth! It is impossible! He is the one white soul in the country. I am bad enough, but we bad men know when a man is good through and through. Often my men and I have stood in the crowd whilst He was speaking, and have been almost persuaded to turn over a new leaf! And *He* is going to die instead of *me*!'

By this time Barabbas has reached the prison entrance. He is saluted by a mass of welcome, and perhaps carried shoulder-high, the idol of the mob. But when they let him go, would he not hasten to the city, replace his prison garb by civilian clothes, remove from his person the traces of the prison, and then make for the scene of crucifixion, so altered as to be hardly recognisable? We see him standing before that central cross, after exchanging glances and words with the two other sufferers. He says to himself: 'That's where I ought to have been, and I deserved it; but I am free and He is suffering in my stead my sentence and my pain.' I have often thought that that sight led him to a new life, that he was converted on the Day of Pentecost, and that he will be conspicuous amid those in heaven who have washed their robes and made them white in the Blood of the Lamb.

The Cross Stands for Substitution

Christ died for the race. He bare our sins in His own body on the tree. He was made sin for us that we might be made God's righteousness in Him. He, the Sinless One, who lived in the sphere of life, holiness, peace, and love, voluntarily stepped down into connection with our fallen race, and undertook by His identification with it to bear our just penalty, and stroke, and doom. He was numbered with the transgressors and bare the sin of the many, and made intercession for the transgressors. 'The sinless last Adam gathered the entire sinful race of the first Adam in His arms, and took them to Calvary.' The stroke fell on Him and all whom He embraced, and His work is complete for all mankind. Because He possessed uncreated Life, he could go down into the sphere of Death and rise above it, taking with Him all those who by patient continuance in well-doing seek for glory, and honour, and incorruption. Even people who have never heard of that wonderful redemption may hereafter participate in it (Romans 2:12-16). But for us all there is the danger of contracting out, as the servant contracted out of his Lord's forgiveness (Matthew 18:28-34). But if you do contract out, you should at least say, 'I thank Thee' to Christ before turning your back on His effort to save you and plunging into eternity 'on your own'!

Before going another step, will you stand before the Cross and say these three sentences, thoughtfully and thankfully:

'He bare *my* sins in His own body on the tree.'

'He loved *me*; He gave Himself for *me*.'

'He was wounded for *my* transgressions, bruised for *my* iniquities, the chastisement of *my* peace was upon Him, and with His stripes *I* am healed.'

Sin has built up a wall between our hearts and God; but in Jesus Christ that wall has been thrown down once for all, and now there is nothing to keep us apart except our own blindness and pride. If only we will turn around and open our hearts to Him; if only we will accept the position He offers us, and which is already ours in Christ, there will be nothing to prevent our lives experiencing everything that the father in the parable was prepared to do for his son. All this is implied in the cords that bind us to the altar!

But the Cross Stands Also for Separation

It is not enough to reach out our hands to receive the forgiveness of our sins, and then to live as we like. To obviate such an inference the Apostles are always insisting on our identification with Christ. Everything that is predicated of Christ is true of us, who, by faith, have become identified with Him. In the thought of eternity we were in Him when He died. In Him we arose, alive unto God; in Him we were raised, as He ascended above all the powers of hell; in Him we are accepted and beloved. The whole New Testament assumes this. 'As you died with Christ to the elemental spirit of the world, why live as if you still belong to the world? ... since, then, you have been raised with Christ, aim at what is above, where Christ is seated at the right hand of God. You died and your life is hidden with Christ in God' (Moffatt: Colossians 2:20; 3:1, 3). 'Surrender your very selves to God as living men who have risen from the dead, and surrender your several faculties to God, to be used as weapons to maintain the right!' (Romans 6:13). 'We become one with Him by sharing His Death; we shall also be one with Him by sharing His Resurrection', not in the hereafter, but now in our present life (Weymouth: Romans 6:5).

There can be no doubt that, in the view of the great teachers of the Church, she is regarded as separated from the world, which cast out the Son of God, and as living on the Pentecostal side of the Cross. This will greatly help us in deciding doubtful matters. Of course we have, like our Lord during His earthly life, to mix with men, to conduct our businesses, to play our part in grave crises; but our behaviour is guided by a spirit and by principles which emanate from our union with the risen and ascended Saviour. Then we understand that the principles laid down in the Sermon on the Mount are those which He uttered as 'the Word of God', and are of eternal importance. Probably, also, they can only become the working principles of daily behaviour when we are living in the enjoyment of those heavenly influences which belong to the Pentecostal age and in the energy of the Holy Spirit.

This thought will help to the solution of many difficult problems. A young girl, who had become a true disciple of Christ and had partaken of the Communion and was teaching in our Sunday School, brought me an invitation which she had received for an evening of fashionable and frivolous amusement. Now, I heartily believe in all rational recreation and amusement, and in our own Church we have fostered whatever would make a healthy mind in a healthy body. Bright happy faces, high spirits, dexterity in games and sport - all these are consistent, as I believe, with true Christianity. The only caution to be added is that they are means to an end, and not the end. In the present case, however, I had to introduce another fact to my young friend, on which it was necessary that she, not I, should decide her action; for is not the Divine Spirit constantly presenting these problems in order to exercise our judgment, and lead us, on our dead selves, to step up to higher things? I, therefore, drew on paper the Cross. On the left hand I wrote the words, 'The World and the Flesh'; on the right the words, 'Ascension and Pentecost'. At the foot of the Cross I drew an oblong representing the Grave. Then I said, 'Under which of these shall I put this invitation?' In order to test her I wrote it on the right hand, along with the Ascension. 'No,' she said, 'it will not do there.' I tried to put it next the crown of thorns, which hung upon the Cross; then next the Grave; but in each case she saw the incongruity, and finally, at her own request, I wrote the word on the left hand under 'The World and the Flesh'. She now saw that, if she accepted, she would have to pass from Resurrection ground backwards through the Grave for a stolen excursion to the world's side of the Cross from which she had been redeemed.

But, for the most part, the redeemed lose their taste for the things that once charmed them. The old Greek myth tells of the siren sisters, who by their songs allured sailors from their course to their doom. Ulysses saved his crew by tying his sailors to their seats, while he with stopped ears steered the boat. But Orpheus did better. He sang so sweetly as to overpower and drown the siren-songs. The latter is the way of Christ. Those who follow Him do not walk in darkness, but have the Light of life; and with that light they become oblivious to the lights of the cruel wreckers along the beach. A young working-girl, speaking of a certain form of amusement, said: 'I went every evening as soon as I had had my tea; I thought I couldn't live without it; but when I found Jesus, and He found me, I lost all my taste for it. I went the other night to see what it was that had held me, but I came out in ten minutes, and shall never go again.'

Surely the Scripture says truly: 'Old things are passed away; behold, all things are become new'. To this, also, our cords bind us, but it is to secure our perfect freedom.

The Cross Also Stands as the Gate of Fuller Life

It was so with Christ Himself: 'Having been made perfect through death, He became the Author of Eternal Salvation to them who obey Him.' It was so with Paul: 'To us who are being saved the word of the Cross is the power of God' (Romans 1:16).

The grave difficulty with us all is the *Ego* which has its seat in the soul-life. The Apostle calls it *the Flesh*. He says: 'In me, that is, in my flesh' (Romans 7:18). Clearly, then, in his nomenclature the flesh is *me*! Spell flesh backwards dropping the 'h' - *s-e-l-f*. We are now dealing not with *Selfishness* but with *Self-ness*. We realise that there is the constant obtrusion of Self in our most hallowed exercises. Even when we are singing God's praises, we are inclined to think how well we can do it, and in our most earnest appeals to men to come to Christ we are tempted to admire our earnestness, or to look back with self-satisfaction on the number of conversions. Sometimes we are tempted to be proud of our humility, and to congratulate ourselves on our knowledge of divine things. The disguises and chameleon-colours of the self-life deceive even the elect.

Dr Tauler, Luther's predecessor, was a very learned and eloquent man. All Strasburg hung on his words, and he was somewhat startled, and perhaps rather annoyed, when Nicolas of Basle crossed the mountains to say, 'Dr Tauler, you must die'. But his resentment became repentance, as his faithful monitor showed him, as in a glass, his real self, proud of his learning, popularity, and insight into the truth.

Finally he left his pulpit, retired for meditation and heart-searching, and learnt the secret of humility and selflessness at the Cross. When he returned and resumed his ministry, though he offended the high and learned, he preached sermons that live today in their English translation as high models of a devout and helpful ministry.

In the person of our Lord the likeness of our sinful flesh was nailed to the Cross. God sent His own Son in a body like that of sinful human nature, and by dying He pronounced sentence upon it. (See Dr Weymouth's translation of Romans 8:3.) God therefore has condemned the I-life, has counted it a felon, has condemned it to eternal condemnation and crucifixion. Whenever, therefore, the 'I' intrudes, we must at once consign it to its proper place. We must treat it as a criminal. Many voices will cry, 'Come down from the Cross', but we must not heed. 'They that are Christ's have crucified the flesh with its affections and lusts.'

But, you say, it is impossible to live like this. You fear that it may induce a harmful introspection and a morbid sensitiveness. But there is no fear of either, if you only remember that you have to hand over all that to the Holy Spirit. Whilst you are occupied with Christ, His voice, His personality, His love and grace, the Holy Spirit who reveals Him will see to the other side of this great process. It was by the Eternal Spirit that Christ offered Himself without spot to God, and it is by the Eternal Spirit that the flesh, or the self-life, is going to be kept to the Cross.

'If ye *through the Spirit* do mortify the deeds of the body, ye shall live.' 'The Spirit lusteth against the flesh.' Keep in touch with the Holy Spirit, occupy yourself with Christ, and the Blessed Paraclete will do the rest. This attitude also will be effected by our fourfold cords!

> '*God forbid that I should glory, save in the Cross of our Lord Jesus Christ.*'

The Cross, it standeth fast, Hallelujah!
Defying every blast, Hallelujah!
The winds of hell have blown,
The world its hate has shown,
Yet it is not overthrown:
Hallelujah, for the Cross!

7

'Filled with the Holy Ghost'
(Luke 1:15, 17)

What may not one man do in one brief life, if he is willing to be simply a living conduit-pipe through which the power of God may descend to men? There is no limit to the possible usefulness of such a life. There, in the one hand, is the oceanic fulness of God; here, on the other, are the awful need and desolation of man, guilty, weak, bankrupt, diseased: all that is required is a channel of communication between the two; and when that channel is made and opened, and kept free from the silting sand, there will ensue one great, plenteous, and equable flow of power carrying the fulness of God to the weary emptiness of man. Why shouldest thou not be such a channel, my reader?

There is a splendid illustration of this in the life of Elijah. For more than a hundred years the tide had been running strongly against the truth of God. Idolatry had passed from the worship of Jeroboam's calves to that of Baal and Astarte; with the licentious orgies and hideous rites which gathered around the ancient worship of the forces of Nature. The system was maintained by an immense organisation of wily priests, who had settled down upon the national life like a fungus growth, striking its roots into the heart. The court was in its favour. The throne was occupied by an effeminate man, the weak tool of his unscrupulous and beautiful wife - the Lady Macbeth of Jewish history. Jehovah's altars were thrown down; His prophets silenced and in hiding; His faithful worshippers a mere handful, whose existence was so secret as to be known only to Him. The lamp of truth had been overturned; and there was only a tiny spark of light feebly burning, to show where once the light of true religion brightly shone.

Into such a state of things Elijah came, unarmed, from his native Trans-Jordanic hills; a highlander, unkempt, unpolished; unaccustomed to the manners of a court, or the learning of the schools. Withal a man weak where we are weak; tempted where we are tempted; of like passions with ourselves. And at once the tide began to turn. The progress of idolatry received a decisive check. The existence and power of Jehovah were vindicated. New courage was infused into the timid remnant of true-hearted disciples. Altars were rebuilt; colleges were opened for the training of the godly youth; a successor was appointed; and an impetus given to the cause of truth, which was felt for many generations.

Perhaps the greatest tribute to Elijah's power with his contemporaries is in the fact that his name and work stood out in bold and clear outline for nine hundred years after his death; surpassing the whole school of Jewish prophets, as the Jungfrau rears her snow-clad peaks above the giants of her chain; and furnishing a model with which to set forth the power and courage of the forerunner of our Lord. The Holy Spirit, speaking in Malachi the last of the prophets, could find no better symbol of the pioneer of the Christ than to compare him with the famous prophet who, centuries before, had swept to heaven in the chariot of flame: 'Behold, I will send you Elijah the prophet before the great and terrible day of the Lord come'. The bright angel Gabriel, standing four hundred years later amid the ascending

69

incense of the holy place, found no easier method of conveying to the aged priest the type of the wondrous son that was to gladden his old age, than to liken him to Elijah. 'He shall go before His face in the spirit and power of Elijah.'

Whenever a notable religious movement was stirring through the land, the people were accustomed to think that the prophet of Carmel had again returned to earth; and thus the deputation asked John the Baptist, saying, 'Art thou Elijah?' and when a mightier than John had set all men musing in their hearts, as the disciples told our Lord, many of the common people believed that the long expectation of centuries was realised, and that Elijah was risen again. It was commonly believed that no other of woman born was great enough to precede the Messiah; and that he would anticipate His advent by an interval of three days, during which he should proclaim, in a voice heard over all the earth - peace, happiness and salvation.

All these things are evidences of the towering greatness of Elijah's character and work. With all the failures and mistakes to which such natures are prone, he was a great man, and did a noble work. And the secret of all was to be found, not in any intrinsic qualities, but in the fact that he was filled with the Holy Ghost. Let us pause here, and ask ourselves if we can give our thoughtful assent to this statement. If we can, we may resolve that we will never rest until we too are filled with the Holy Ghost. We will not rest satisfied in being imitators merely; but we will seek to be filled with the same Spirit, that He may work again through us the marvels of the past.

If I may venture so to put it, God is in extremity for men who, thoughtless for themselves, will desire only to be receivers and channels of His power. He will take young men and women, old men and children, servants and handmaidens, in the waning days of this era, and will fill them with the selfsame Spirit whose power was once reserved for a favoured few. Besides all this, the positive command has never been repealed which bids us be 'filled with the Spirit' (Ephesians 5:18). And we cannot reiterate too often that those who feel themselves bound to strict temperance in respect to wine by the former clause, should feel the latter one to be equally imperative. Moreover, what God commands, He is prepared to do all that is needful on His side to effect. Then when, like John the Baptist, we are filled with the Holy Ghost, like John the Baptist we shall go 'before His face in the spirit and power of Elijah; to turn the hearts of the fathers to the children, and the disobedient to walk in the wisdom of the just; to make ready for the Lord a people prepared for Him'.

(1) This filling of the Holy Ghost was the characteristic of the Church

On the day of Pentecost they were *all* filled with the Holy Ghost - women as well as men; obscure disciples as well as illustrious apostles; and to guard against the leakage which is alas too common to us all, they were filled and filled again; those who are described as filled in Acts 2:4 are spoken of as filled again in Acts 4:31. New converts, like Saul of Tarsus, were bidden to expect this blessed filling. Deacons called to do the secular business of the Church must be men filled with the Holy Ghost. That he was a good man, full of the Holy Ghost, was a greater recommendation of Barnabas than that he had parted with his lands. And even churches, like those in the highlands of Galatia, were no sooner brought into existence by the labours of the Apostle Paul than they were filled with the Holy Ghost. In point of fact, the Christians of the first age were taught to expect this blessed filling. And the early Church was a collection of Holy Ghost-filled people. Probably it was the exception, rather than the rule, *not* to be filled with the blessed presence of God the Holy Ghost.

There is no formal conclusion to the Acts of the Apostles; because God meant the story to be prolonged, through the ages, after the same manner. Let us not think that God resembles some who put a portico of marble to a building which they finish with common brick. He did not give at Pentecost an experience which He either would not or could not maintain. Pentecost was simply meant to be the specimen and type of all the days of all the years of the present age. And if our times seem to have fallen far below this blessed level, it is not because of any failure on God's part; but because the Church has neglected this holy doctrine. Christians have seemed to suppose that the filling of the Holy Ghost was the prerogative of a few; the majority of them have never thought of it as within their reach; and the Church has been simply paralysed for want of the only power that can avail her in her conflict against the world - a power which was distinctly pledged to her by her ascending Lord.

We never can regain or hold our true position until all believers see that the filling of the Holy Ghost is equally for them as for the first Christians; and that the barriers are broken down which once limited it to a few. We do not seek the sound of rushing wind; or the coronet of flame; or the special gifts which were conferred for a special purpose: these are the minor accessories of this filling, with which

72

we can dispense. But what we cannot dispense with, and must not dream of missing, is - the distinct filling of the Holy Ghost. No doubt He is in us if we are Christians; but we must never be content until He is in us in power - not a breath, but a mighty wind; not a rill, but a torrent; not an influence, but a mighty, energising Person.

(2) We must comply with certain conditions, if we would be filled
(a) We must desire to be filled for the glory of God. A lady told me lately that she had long been seeking the power of the Spirit, but in vain. She could not understand the cause of her failure, till she came to see that she was seeking Him for the joy that He would bring, rather than for the glory that would accrue to God. Ah, we must seek for the Spirit's power, not for our happiness or comfort, nor yet for the good that we may be the better able to effect; but that 'Christ may be magnified in our bodies, whether by life or death'.

(b) We must bring cleansed vessels. God will not deposit His most precious gift in unclean receptacles. And we need cleansing in the precious blood, ere we can presume to expect that God will give us what we seek. We cannot expect to be free from indwelling sin; but we may at least be washed in the blood of Christ from all conscious filthiness and stain.

(c) We must be prepared to let the Holy Spirit do as He will with and through us. There must be no reserve; no holding back; no contrariety of purpose. The whole nature must be unbarred, and every part yielded. There is a law in physics that forces work in the direction of least resistance. Let us present no resistance whatever to the working of the

73

Holy Ghost. He who resists least will possess most. God gives the Holy Ghost to them that obey Him (Acts 5:32).

(d) We must appropriate Him by faith. There is no need for us to wait ten days, because the Holy Spirit *has been given* to the church. This is included in the spiritual blessings with which our Father *hath* blessed us in Christ Jesus. We need not struggle, and agonise, and convulse ourselves in the vehemence of entreaty; we have simply to take what God has allotted to us, and is waiting to impart. Open your mouth wide, and He will fill it. Dig the ditches; and though you can discern no evidences of the entering floods, they shall be filled. Ask as a little child asks for its breakfast already on the table. So soon as you ask, you do receive, though you experience no rush of transcendent joy; go your way reckoning yourself filled, whether you feel so or not; and as the days go on, you will find that you have been filled, and are being filled, with new power and joy, and wealth. You will not long be left to the reckoning of faith; for you will be made aware of a virtue going out from you, which shall heal and save.

(3) Time would fail to enumerate all the blessings that will ensue

The presence of the Holy Ghost in the heart, in all His glorious fulness, cannot be hid. It will surely betray itself, as the presence of the ever-burning fire in the hot-house is indicated by the luxuriance of flower and fruit within its tropical enclosure, whilst frost and snow reign in the world without. There will be no effort; no striving after great effect; no ostentatious show. He distils as the dew upon the tender herb; and descends as the summer showers upon the mown grass. This conception of His work is clearly taught by the word selected by the Apostle to describe the results of His indwelling. He speaks of them as the '*fruit* of the Spirit', in contrast to the '*works* of the flesh'; and what deep suggestions of quiet growth, and exquisite beauty, and spontaneousness of life lie in that significant phrase!

In passing, we can do no more than enumerate some of the results of the indwelling of the Holy Ghost.

There is victory over sin. The law of the Spirit of life in Christ Jesus makes us free from the law of sin and death; just as the law of the elasticity of the air makes the bird free from the predominating power of the down-pull of gravitation.

There is the indwelling of the Lord Jesus. Christ dwells in the heart by the Holy Ghost; so that there are not two indwellings, but one. And this not figurative or metaphorical, but a literal and glorious reality.

There is the quickening of the mortal body. An expression which certainly points to the Resurrection; but which may mean some special strength and health imparted to our present mortal bodies - the tabernacles and temples of His indwelling.

There are all the graces of the Spirit, which come with linked hands; so that it is impossible to admit one of the golden sisterhood without her introducing all the radiant band. Love brings joy; and joy peace; and peace long-suffering; and similarly through the whole series: so that the heart becomes at length tenanted, as was the grave of Christ, with angels.

There is also power for service. No longer timid and frightened, the Apostles give their witness with great power. The gospel comes in power and demonstration through consecrated lips and lives. The very devils are exorcised; and great crowds are brought to the feet of Christ.

This, and much more, is awaiting the moment in thy life, my reader, when thou shalt definitely avail thyself of thy privilege and become filled with the Holy Ghost. Then as time rolls on, thou shalt work great deliverances among men, careless of praise or blame. Perhaps thou shalt know what it is to pass upward to meet Christ in the air. But certainly thou shalt stand beside Him in the regeneration when He shall appear in glory. And then in all the radiant throng there shall be nought to divert thy gaze from 'Jesus only'; or thy thought from the decease (the exodus) which He accomplished at Jerusalem.

And amid the myriads of stars that shall shine for ever in the firmament of heaven, not one shall sparkle with more brilliant or more steady glory than Elijah; a man of like passions with ourselves, who through faith subdued kingdoms, wrought righteousness, obtained promises, out of weakness was made strong, waxed valiant in fight, swept to heaven unhurt by death, and stood beside Christ on the Transfiguration Mount. Prophet of Fire, till then, Farewell!

8

A Fisher of Men
(Luke 5:8-11)

I know not what I am, but only know
I have had glimpses tongue may never speak;
No more I balance human joy and woe,
But think of my transgressions and am weak.

(Buchanan)

The Master's purpose for His disciples is disclosed in the words recorded by Matthew and Mark, and which were probably addressed to them on the shore, when they had again beached their boats: 'Come ye after Me, and I will make you to become fishers of men'. We can combine this form of the summons with that specially addressed to the impulsive, vehement, warm-hearted son of Jonas, and which is recorded in Luke 5. It should be noticed that here, as generally in the Gospels, our Lord addresses him by the more intimate name of *Simon*, as though *Peter* were reserved till, through the months of discipline which awaited him, he was fitted to take the foremost place among his fellow apostles.

The summons came whilst they were engaged in their usual occupation. David was summoned from the sheep-fold to shepherd the chosen race. Paul was called from making the goat's hair tents to teach the Church the ephemeral character of the things that are seen, in view of the house not made with hands, eternal in the heavens. The eternal springs were revealed to the woman as she rested her pitcher on the embrasure of Jacob's well. It was quite befitting, therefore, that our Lord should explain to his fisher friend the momentous and glorious ministry that awaited him, through the calling in which he had been engaged from boyhood, and which had so many points of resemblance with the work of winning souls. The one difference being brought out in the Greek word translated *catch*, and which should be expanded to read, as in 2 Timothy 2:26, 'Thou shalt catch, *in order to keep alive*'.

In every subsequent era sincere and earnest souls have lingered wistfully over these words, longing to extract from them the precious secret of successful soul-winning. More than two hundred years ago, Thomas Boston, a young Scots minister, made this record in his diary: 'Reading in secret, my heart was touched with these words, *Thou shalt catch men*. My soul cried out for their accomplishing in me, and I was very desirous to know how I might follow Christ, so as to be a fisher of men; and for my own instruction I addressed myself to the consideration of that point.'

It would be tedious to enumerate the various suggestions that have been made on the line of Boston's treatise, which was entitled *A Soliloquy on the Art of Man-fishing*. Many a godly minister with a perfectly-appointed Church, and surrounded by a devoted people - the boat, the company, and the fishing-tackle being all of the best - has watched, almost enviously, the success of some simple evangelist who, apart from all adventitious aid, has lifted netfuls of fish from the great depths of human life into his creel. One expert fisherman says: 'Keep yourself out of sight'. Another urges that the bait and method must be carefully adapted to the habits of the fish. Yet a third insists on patience. What success is gained by scourging the water! All are good, but the study of this narrative may bring us still further into the heart of the matter and the mind of our Lord.

(1) Successful soul-winning is generally based on a deep consciousness of personal sinnership

Many instances present themselves from the biographies of the saints. But two will suffice. The untiring and extraordinary labours of the great Apostle of the Gentiles laid the foundations of the Gentile Church, but as he reviews the past and considers his natural condition, he does not hesitate to speak of himself as the chief of sinners and the least of saints. We faint not, he says, because the grace of God displayed its exceeding riches in our redemption. 'We all once lived in the lusts of our flesh, fulfilling the desires of the flesh and of the mind, and were by nature children of wrath, even as the rest'. John Bunyan's review of his condition, as it stood revealed in the light of God, is typical of many others, who shine as stars in the firmament of successful soul-winning. He says, 'I was more loathsome in mine own eyes than was a toad; and I thought I was so in God's eyes also. I could have changed my heart with anyone. I thought none but the devil himself could equal me for inward wickedness and pollution of mind. I was both a burden and a terror to myself. How gladly would I have been anything but myself.'

Those who have had deep experiences of the exceeding sinfulness of sin are the better qualified to be tender and pitiful to such as are sold under sin, are heaping up for themselves agonies of remorse against the day of their awakening, are causing infinite sorrow to the Saviour, and are missing the great purposes for which they were created.

'Alas, poor souls!' they cry, 'such were some of us.' The ringleaders in the devil's army make great soldiers for Christ. Their knowledge of Satan's stratagems and wiles is invaluable. Reclaimed poachers are notoriously the best gamekeepers. The sinner knows the bitterness of the wages of sin, as an unfallen angel or an innocent child cannot. Men like Augustine or Bunyan have learnt by experience the subterfuges and evasions of conscience, the horror of remorse, the yearning for help. They are familiar with the holes where the fish lie, and the best methods of reaching them. They have infinite patience, as the Lord had patience with them. They bear gently with the erring, and with those who resent their approach, because they themselves have been compassed with infirmity. We are sometimes tempted to say with Augustine, *O beata culpa* (Oh, blessed fault!), because the knowledge of our own sinful hearts gives us the clue to all other hearts oppressed by temptation. We need not be surprised, therefore, at this preparatory revelation of Himself given to Peter.

He and the rest had known the Lord for at least eighteen months, but were unaware of His true majesty and glory. For them He was the carpenter of Nazareth, the holy man, the marvellous teacher and wonder-worker. That He was, like the Baptist, a chosen servant of God and the herald of a new era was their common conclusion. Beyond this their minds had not travelled. They regarded Jesus as of the same flesh and blood with themselves, felt glad to be honoured with His friendship, and were pleased in return to share with Him their slender stores or humble homes. It never occurred to them that they were in daily touch with the Lamb that was slain before the worlds were made, or that for their reception He had emptied Himself, made Himself of no reputation, and assumed the form of a servant.

Then most suddenly and unexpectedly this shaft of His essential being struck into their ordinary commonplace, and left a trail of supernatural glory. For a moment Peter was dazzled, almost blinded. He could hardly see for the splendour of that light; but as he felt the tug and pull of the bursting net, threatening to break beneath its sudden burden, he realised in a moment that his Teacher and Friend must have put forth a power which no mortal could wield. God was in the place, and he had not known it. How dreadful was that place! It was none other than the house of God and the gate of heaven; and at once the nakedness and sinfulness of his own heart were laid bare, and he cried: 'I am a sinful man, O Lord'. Note the significant exchange! When the boat left the shore it was *Master*, now, as this revelation has broken on him, it is *Lord*. Immediately on this Jesus said: 'From henceforth thou shalt catch men.'

There is a striking analogy between Peter's experience and Job's. The suffering patriarch had persistently and successfully maintained his integrity. 'Till I die I will not remove mine integrity from me. My righteousness will I hold fast. I will not let it go. My heart shall not reproach me as long as I live.' Then into his life God let fall visions of the Creation. He recited instance after instance of His almighty power, wisdom and skill. As Peter's eyes were unveiled that he might behold Christ's wonders in the deep, so were Job's; and he exclaimed, as the divine glory shone upon his soul, 'I have heard of Thee by the hearing of the ear, but now mine eye seeth Thee, wherefore I abhor myself and repent in dust and ashes.'

Oh agony of wavering thought
When sinners first so near are brought.
'It is my Maker! - dare I stay?
My Saviour! - dare I turn away?'

Whenever, therefore, this experience befalls, it may be deemed as preparatory to new success in soul-winning. Expect to hear the Lord answer your confession of lowly sinnership with a new summons to take your boat and net for a draught. And this experience does and will befall, not once or twice, but many times, as we approach nearer to the Alpine snows of our Lord's unsullied holiness. The whole progress of the divine life within the soul is characterised by confessions. We are always being led to detect the presence of sin and evil in depths and motions, which once seemed comparatively harmless and innocent. The true soul is always counting its righteousnesses as filthy rags, and confessing that it has not yet attained nor is by any means perfect. The only confession that befits us is that we are following after to apprehend that for which we were apprehended of Christ Jesus. The higher the flight of the soaring eagle the deeper its reflection in the mountain-lake. Do not be afraid to know yourself beneath the Spirit's teaching, it is all preparatory to a new departure in 'man-catching'.

(2) Failure and Sin do not necessarily exclude from the Divine Partnership in soul-winning

'Depart from me,' cried the conscience-stricken disciple. It was as though he said: 'I will bring Thee, Lord, to the spot where I took Thee on board this morning; and when I have landed Thee, Thou must go Thy way and I mine. I shall ever love Thee and think of Thee as I float under these skies by day and night, but I am not fit to keep Thee company.' And under his breath he may have whispered to himself: 'But I know not how I shall live without Thee. To whom can I turn? Thou only hast the words of eternal life.'

We can almost see him, when the well of the boat was heaped high with the slippery silver cargo, clambering across from prow and stern on his bare feet, falling at Jesus' knees as He sat near the tiller, clasping them, and faltering forth these words with the heaving sobs of a strong man torn with conflicting emotions.

It was as though our King Alfred, when wandering in Sherwood Forest, disguised, lost to his followers, and uncertain as to the path, had been found and befriended by a kindly woodsman, who had regarded him as an equal, shared with him his bed and board without detecting his royal dignity, and finally had conveyed him to his brave retainers. How startled he would be to see their deferential respect! Suddenly he would awake to the vast chasm intervening between himself and his ward, and approaching with many apologies for his familiarity, would deferentially propose to say goodbye and farewell for ever. 'Our paths, sire, must of course diverge from this point! You to your throne, I to my cottage!'

'Nay,' said our Lord in effect, 'that need not be. When sin is repented of, abhorred, and confessed, it need not debar from My presence or service. I can do with sinful men, who are conscious of their sinnership. No sin is too inveterate but that I can cope with it, too foul but that I can cleanse. Stay with Me, I will cleanse, heal, and save thee, and make thee the instrument of saving thousands of sinners like thyself.'

It is impossible to exaggerate the comfort that these

words afford to those who would fain serve Christ, though conscious of their profound unworthiness. 'I am not worthy to bear the message of salvation to others, because I am such a sinful man! How canst Thou employ me, who hast hosts of unfallen angels at Thy command? How darest Thou identify Thyself and Thy holy cause with me? No, it cannot be! I love Thee, but an ever-widening river must divide us as we walk on either bank. I shall break my heart that I have failed Thee so, but I cannot lift up my face, or regain my forfeited place. Let me stand in the outer circle and see Thee now and again. I cannot ask for more, for Thou knowest, and I know, and every lost spirit knows, that I am a sinful man.'

But Jesus has only one reply: 'Fear not, from henceforth thou shalt catch men.' 'Fear not! I am the Daysman that stands as thy surety. I have blotted out thy transgressions as a cloud, and will no more remember thy sins. I have loved thee with an everlasting love, though I foresaw all this and more also. Depart from Me! It is unthinkable. Thou art dearer to Me than all the stars in their galaxies. I have obtained from the Father that thou shouldst be with Me, where I am. After thou hast had thy Pentecost, and fulfilled thy ministry and finished thy course, thou shalt be accounted worthy to stand in My Presence-chamber, that thou mayest behold My glory, and thou shalt share it.'

'Lord, it is too much; let me kiss Thy feet!'

(3) Soul-winning, to be successful, must be the absorbing of our lives

It cannot be one interest among many. The Apostle said truly, 'One thing I do.' 'They left all and followed Him.' We can imagine that after this moving exchange of words

Peter returned to his place to think over the marvel of the life that now opened before him. And whilst he mused, the fire burned. What else was worth living for? Surely he must obey this mandate. 'Come ye after me!' 'Hither, follow!'

May we indulge our imagination here? The boat responds to sail or oar, and makes for the shore. A friendly fisherman informs his wife that the well-known boat will soon be 'in'. His food has been waiting for him since early dawn. She had prepared a breakfast for which he did not come. She hastens to the shore and stands there with her welcome, all the gladder because she descries its burden. Her husband leaps into the shallow water and lifts Jesus from boat to beach. He then approaches her wistfully, and with an unwonted tenderness that startles her, 'Can you spare me for a little?' he inquires. 'The Master has asked me to go with Him. He says that I am not to fear, and that He will provide for us. He has promised to teach me how to fish for men. I will come back as soon as I have learned my lesson and He has done with me. In the meanwhile I must be free to serve Him. Can you spare me?'

And she replies: 'Husband, go with Him. Mother and I will make shift somehow till you get back. Stay with Him as long as He needs you. Mother and I were saying only this morning that you have been a different man since you knew Him.'

She came to believe also, and travelled everywhere with her husband, helping him, as Paul bears witness (1 Corinthians 9:5). We cannot suppose that Peter at once entered into the Master's passion for the souls of men. That was acquired afterwards. In the first instance he was content to follow *Him*, to listen to His words, to become His companion and helper. But it could not have been long before he and his companions began to be imbued with the same passion, until it became the master-motive of their existence.

So it will be with ourselves. As we walk with Christ, by the constant aid of the Holy Spirit, we shall be conformed to His image. His thoughts and yearnings will be transmitted to us by a Divine sympathy. We shall long to see Him honoured, loved and exalted. We shall desire that He shall see of the travail of His soul and be satisfied. We shall become identified with His interests, and with no backward look on ourselves. The Holy Spirit will blow these sparks into a flame, and our life will be spent as that of Peter, who by his love for Christ was qualified to feed His sheep and lambs.

Let us ask that we may become partners with Christ in His great passion for men. Let us bring ourselves to this great magnet till we are magnetised. Oh to be a living flame for Jesus Christ, so that the uttermost love of a woman may be:

Faint to the flame with which our breast is burning,
Less than the love wherewith we ache for souls!

9

The Sin of David's Life
(2 Samuel 11-19)

'O Father, I have sinned! I have done
The thing I thought I never more should do!
My days were set before me, light all through;
But I have made dark - alas, too true! -
And drawn dense clouds between me and my Sun.'
                                    (Septimus Sutton)

The chronicler omits all reference to this terrible blot on
David's life. The older record sets down each item without
extenuation or excuse. The gain for all penitents would so
much outweigh the loss to the credit of the man after God's
own heart. These chapters have been trodden by myriads
who, having well-nigh lost themselves in the same dark
labyrinth of sin, have discovered the glimmer of light by
which the soul may pass back into the day. 'Thy sins, which
are many, are forgiven thee; go in peace.'

(1) The circumstances that led to David's sin
The warm poetic temperament of the king specially ex-
posed him to a temptation of this sort; but the self-re-
strained habit of his life would have prevailed, had there
not been some slackening of the loin, some failure to trim
the lamp.

For seventeen years he had enjoyed an unbroken spell
of prosperity; in every war successful, on every great
occasion increasing the adulation of his subjects. This was

fraught with peril. The rigours of the Alps are less to be dreaded than the heat of the enervating plains of the Campagna.

In direct violation of the law of Moses - which forbade the multiplication of wives on the part of Hebrew kings, 'lest their hearts should turn away' - we are distinctly told that, when established at Jerusalem, David took unto him more concubines and wives; sowing to himself the inevitable harvest of heart-burning, jealousy, quarrelling, and crime, of which the harem must also be the prolific source, besides fostering in David himself a habit of sensual indulgence, which predisposed him to the evil solicitation of that evening hour.

He had also yielded to a fit of indolence, unlike the martial spirit of the Lion of Judah; allowing Joab and his brave soldiers to do the fighting around the walls of Rabbah, while he tarried still at Jerusalem. It was a mood to which Uriah administered a stinging rebuke when he refused to go to his own house whilst his comrades and the Ark were encamped on the open field.

One sultry afternoon the king had risen from his afternoon siesta, and was lounging on his palace-roof. In that hour of enervated ease, to adopt Nathan's phrase, a traveller came to him, a truant thought, to satisfy whose hunger he descended into the home of a poor man and took his one ewe lamb, although his own folds were filled with flocks. We will not extenuate his sin by dwelling on Bathsheba's willing complicity, or on her punctilious ceremonial purification; while she despised her plighted married troth to her absent husband. The Scripture record lays the burden of the sin on the king alone, before whose absolute power Bathsheba may have felt herself obliged to yield.

One brief spell of passionate indulgence, and then! - his character blasted irretrievably; his peace vanished; the foundations of his kingdom imperilled; the Lord displeased; and great occasion given to his enemies to blaspheme! Let us beware of our light, unguarded hours. Moments of leisure are more to be dreaded than those of strenuous toil. Middle life - for David was above fifty years of age - has no immunity from temptations and perils which beset the young. One false step taken in the declension of spiritual vigour may ruin a reputation built up by years of religious exercise.

A message came one day to David from his companion in sin that the results could not be hidden. It made his blood run with hot fever. The law of Moses punished adultery with the death of each of the guilty pair. Instant steps must be taken to veil the sin! Uriah must come home! He came, but his coming did not help the matter. He refused to go to his home, though on the first night the king sent him thither a mess of meat straight from his table, and on the second made him drunk. The chivalrous soul of the soldier shrank even from the greeting of his wife whilst the great war was still in process.

There was no alternative but that he should die; for dead men tell no tales. If a child was to be born, Uriah's lips, at least, should not be able to disown it. He bore to Joab, all unwitting, the letter which was his own death-warrant. Joab must have laughed to himself when he got it. 'This master of mine can sing psalms with the best; but when he wants a piece of dirty work done, he must come to me. He wants to rid himself of Uriah - I wonder why? Well, I'll help him to it. At any rate, he will not be able to say another word to me about Abner. I shall be able to do almost as I will. He will be in my power henceforth.' Uriah was set in the forefront of the hottest battle, and left to die; the significant item of his death being inserted in the bulletin sent to the king from the camp. It was supposed by David that only he and Joab knew of this thing; probably Bathsheba did not guess the costly method by which her character was being protected. She lamented for her dead husband, as was the wont of a Hebrew matron, congratulating herself mean-while on the fortunate coincidence; and within seven days was taken into David's house. A great relief this! The child would be born under the cover of lawful wedlock! There was one fatal flaw, however, in the whole arrangement. 'The thing that David had done displeased the Lord.' David and the world were to hear more of it. But oh, the bitter sorrow, that he who had spoken of walking in his house with a perfect heart, with all his faculty for Divine fellowship, with all the splendid record of his life behind him, should have fallen thus! The psalmist, the king, the man, the lover of God, all trampled in the mire by one dark, wild passionate outburst. Ah me! My God, grant that I may finish my course without such a rent, such a blot! Oh to wear the white flower of a blameless life to the end!

(2) Delayed repentance

The better the man, the dearer the price he pays for a short season of sinful pleasure. For twelve whole months the royal sinner wrapt his sin in his bosom, pursed his lips, and refused to confess. But in Psalm 32 he tells us how he felt. His bones waxed old through his roaring all the day long. He was parched with fever heat, as when in Israel for three years there was neither dew nor rain in answer to Elijah's prayer, and every green thing withered in the awful drought of summer. Day and night God's hand lay heavily upon him.

When he took Rabbah, he treated the people with ferocious cruelty, as if weary of his own remorse, and expending on others the hardness which he ought to have dealt out to himself. We often excuse ourselves from avenging our own sin, by our harsh behaviour and uncharitable judgments towards others. The same spirit, which always characterises the sullen, uneasy conscience, flamed out in his sentence on the rich man who had taken the poor man's lamb. The Levitical law in such a case only adjudged fourfold restoration (Exodus 22:1). The king pronounced sentence of death.

Nathan's advent on the scene must have been a positive relief. One day whilst statesmen and soldiers were crowding the outer corridor of the cedar palace, the prophet, by right of old acquaintance, made his way through them, and sought a private audience. He told what seemed to be a real and pathetic story of high-handed wrong; and David's anger was greatly kindled against the man who had perpetrated it. Then, as a flash of lightning on a dark night suddenly reveals to the traveller the precipice, on the void of which he is about to place his foot, the brief awful stunning sentence, 'Thou art the man!' revealed David to himself in the mirror of his own judgment, and brought him to his knees. Nathan reminded him of the past, and dwelt specially on the unstinted goodness of God. It was a sunny background, the sombre hues of which made recent events look the darker. 'Thou hast despised his word; thou hast slain Uriah; thou hast taken his wife. The child shall die; thy wives shall be treated as thou hast dealt with his; out of thine own house evil shall rise against thee.' 'I have sinned against the Lord,' was David's only answer - a confession followed by a flood of hot tears - and instantly his scorched heart found relief. Oh, blessed showers that visit parched souls and parched lands!

When Nathan had gone, David beat out that brief confession into Psalm 51, dedicated to the chief musician, that all the world might use it, setting it to music if they would. The one sin and the many transgressions; the evil done against God, as though even Uriah might not be named in the same breath; the confession of inbred evil; the ache of the broken bones; the consciousness of the unclean heart; the loss of joy; the fear of forfeiting the Holy Spirit; the broken and contrite heart - thus the surcharged waters of the inner lake broke forth turbid and dark. Ah, those cries for the multitude of God's tender mercies! nothing less could erase the dark legend from the book of remembrance, or rub out the stains from his robe, or make the leprous flesh sweet and whole. To be clean, because purged with hyssop; to be whiter than snow, because washed; to sing aloud once more, because delivered from the blood-guiltiness; to be infilled with a steadfast, a willing, and a holy spirit; to be able to point transgressors to the Father's heart - these were the petitions which that weak, sin-weary heart laid upon the altar of God, sweeter than burnt-offering or fragrant incense.

But long before this pathetic prayer was uttered, immediately on his acknowledgement of sin, without the interposition of a moment's interval between his confession and the assurance, Nathan had said, 'The Lord hath put away thy sin.'

'I acknowledge my sin unto Thee, and mine iniquity
have I not hid.
I said, I will confess my transgressions unto the Lord,
And Thou forgavest the iniquity of my sin.'

Penitent soul! Dare to believe in the instantaneous
forgiveness of sins. Thou hast only to utter the confession,
to find it interrupted with the outbreak of the Father's love.
As soon as the words of penitence leave thy lips, they are
met by the hurrying assurances of a love which, whilst it
hates sin, has never ceased to yearn over the prodigal.

Sin is dark, dangerous, damnable: but it cannot staunch
the love of God; it cannot change the love that is not of
yesterday, but dates from eternity itself. The only thing that
can really hurt the soul is to keep its confession pent within
itself. If only with stuttering, broken utterance it dares to
cry, 'Be merciful to me, the sinner, for the sake of the Blood
that was shed', it instantly becomes white as snow on
Alpine peaks; pure as the waters of mid-ocean, which the
stain of the great city cannot soil; transparent as the blue
ether which is the curtain of the tabernacle of the Most
High.

10

Preparing for Pisgah

*'And Moses said unto them, I am a hundred and twenty years
old this day; I can no more go out and come in: also the Lord
hath said unto me, Thou shalt not go over this Jordan'
(Deuteronomy 31:2).*

Just before the dark River through which Pilgrims pass to
the City of Gold, Bunyan places the land of Beulah; where
the sun ever shines, the birds sing, and every day the
flowers appear on the earth. The air is very sweet and
pleasant. It is within sight of the City, but it is beyond the
reach of Giant Despair; and they who come thither cannot
so much as see the turrets of Doubting Castle. And in some
such blissful experience saintly men have sought to spend
a brief parenthesis between the press of life's business and
their entrance into the welcome of Christ. But such was not
the experience of Moses. The last year of his life was as full
of work as any that had ever passed over his head.

There was, first, the conquest of Eastern Canaan. Dean
Stanley speaks of it as that mysterious eastern frontier of
the Holy Land, so beautiful, so romantic, so little known.
Its original inhabitants had been expelled by the kindred
tribes of Moab and Ammon; but they, in their turn, had
been dispossessed of a considerable portion of the territory
thus acquired, by the two Canaanite chiefs, Sihon and Og,
whose names occur so frequently in this narrative.

The attack of the Israelites was justified by the churlish
refusal of Sihon to the request that they might march

through his borders on their way to Jericho. He not only refused them passage, but gathered all his people together, and went out against Israel on the frontier line between his territory and the wilderness. The song which commemorated the victory lays special emphasis on the prowess of the slingers and archers of Israel, afterwards, so renowned: 'We have shot at them; Heshbon is perished'.

These words suggest the probable reason for the overthrow of this powerful monarch, under the providence of God. The sword followed on arrow or stone, so that the army was practically annihilated; no further resistance was offered to the march of the victorious foe. The cities opened their gates; and this fertile region between the Arnon and the Jabbok, consisting of 'a wide table-land, tossed about in wild confusion of undulating downs, clothed with rich grass, and in spring waving with great sheets of wheat and barley', came into possession of the chosen people.

But this was not all. North of this lay Bashan, which has been described by Canon Tristram and others as a rich and well-wooded country, abounding in noble forests of oak and of olive trees, interspersed with patches of corn in the open glades. It was and is the most picturesque and the most productive portion of the Holy Land. Og, its king, was renowned for his gigantic stature. According to Josephus' narrative, he was coming to the assistance of Sihon, when he heard of his defeat and death. But, undaunted, he set his army in array against the hosts of Israel. The battle took place at Edrei, which stood to guard the entrance of a remarkable mountain fastness; and it ended in the complete victory of Israel. The result is told in the strong, concise narrative of Moses. 'They smote him, his sons, and all his people, until there was none left him remaining; and they possessed his land.'

Nothing could have accounted for the marvellous victories, which gave Israel possession of these valuable tracts of country - with cities fenced with high walls, gates, and bars, together with a great many unwalled towns - but the interposition of God. He had said beforehand, 'Fear not! I have delivered him into thy hand'; and so it befell. Immense swarms of hornets, which are common in Palestine, seemed to have visited the country at this juncture; so that the people were driven from their fortresses into the open plains, where they were less able to stand the assault of the Israelites.

Moses, at their urgent request, proceeded to allot this rich and beautiful territory to the Reubenites and Gadites and the half-tribe of Manasseh, after receiving their solemn pledge to bear their share in the conquest of Western Palestine. 'I commanded you,' he said afterwards, 'that ye shall pass armed before your brethren, the children of Israel, until the Lord give rest unto your brethren, as unto you.'

Next came his last charge to the people. This was delivered in a series of farewell addresses, which are contained in chapters 1-30 of the Book of Deuteronomy. This book is to the four preceding ones much what the Gospel according to John is to the other three. It is full of the most pathetic and stirring appeals. Memory of the past, gratitude, fear, self-interest, are the chords made to vibrate to this master-touch. Well may it be said of Moses that he loved the people; and in these pages we may trace the course of the molten lava which poured from his heart.

The key-phrases of that remarkable book are: Keep

diligently; Observe to do; and, The Lord shall choose. It abounds with exquisite descriptions of the Land of Promise, which may be spiritually applied to those rapturous experiences denoted by the phrase, The Rest of Faith. It is, indeed, as old Canaan was, a good land, a land of brooks of water, of fountains and depths springing out of valleys and hills. There we drink of the river of the water of life; there we eat the bread of life without scarceness and lack nothing that we really need. The 28th chapter anticipates the Beatitudes of our Lord's Sermon on the Mount; and happy is he that can appropriate them in blissful experience, and go in to possess the land.

In our judgment the much-debated question of authorship is settled by the distinct affirmation of the New Testament. Take, for instance, the quotation of Deuteronomy 30:11-14 in Romans 10:6-10. The Apostle Paul distinctly speaks of Moses as having written these words.

Next came his anxiety about a successor. Moses spake unto the Lord, saying, 'Let the Lord, the God of the spirits of all flesh, set a man over the congregation, which may go out before them, and which may go in before them; which may lead them out, and bring them in, that the congregation of the Lord be not as sheep which have no shepherd.' In answer to this request, he had been directed to take Joshua, the son of Nun, in whom was the Spirit, to bring him before Eleazar, the priest, and before all the congregation, and to give him a charge. This he seems to have done; but as death drew near he apparently gave him a second charge (compare Numbers 27:16, 17 and Deuteronomy 31:7, 8).

What a striking scene it must have been when, on his one hundred and twentieth birthday, the aged lawgiver called unto Joshua, and said unto him in the sight of all

Israel, 'Be strong and of a good courage: for thou must go with this people unto the land which the Lord hath sworn unto their fathers to give them; and thou shalt cause them to inherit it. And the Lord, He it is that doth go before thee; He will be with thee; He will not fail thee, neither forsake thee; fear not, neither be dismayed.' Immediately afterwards the pillar of cloud stood over the door of the Tabernacle, and Moses and Joshua were summoned to present themselves before God in its sacred precincts. There, in almost identical words to those which He had spoken by the lips of Moses, God gave Joshua his commission to bring the children of Israel into the land which He had sworn unto them, together with the promise that He would be with them.

His last acts were to arrange for the custody of the Law and the perpetuation of its reading. He did the first by depositing the book, in which he had recorded the Divine revelations made to him, in the side of the Ark of the Covenant. It was to be kept under the custody of the Levites; and passages were to be read from it at the end of every seven years, when all Israel appeared before God in the place which He should choose.

And as to the second, Moses put his exhortations and entreaties into two magnificent odes, the one dealing out warnings against apostasy, the other dwelling seriatim on the characteristics of the tribes, and giving them a parting blessing, after the fashion of the dying Jacob.

The thirty-second chapter of Deuteronomy is one of the sublimest human compositions on record. It was Moses' swan song. It is the store from which later Scripture writers draw plentifully. It has been called the Magna Carta of Prophecy. It is worthy to be compared to one only song else, the Song of the Lamb, with which it is combined by the harpers on the margin of the glassy sea: 'They sing the song of Moses, the servant of God, and the song of the Lamb.'

The repeated comparisons of God to a Rock; the lavish kindness with which He had treated his people since He first found them in a desert land; the comparison of the Eternal to a mother eagle in teaching its young to climb the unaccustomed steeps of air; the ingratitude with which his marvellous kindness had been requited; the dread fate to which their rebellion must expose them; the mercy with which their repentance would be greeted - all these are recorded in glowing, eloquent words, that stand for ever as a witness of how stammering lips may speak when they have been touched with the live altar coal. Or take the closing verses of the Benediction on the tribes. The lonely glory of the God of Jeshurun, who rides on the heavens to help and save his people; the home which men may find in his eternal nature; the underpinning everlasting arms; the irresistible might with which He thrusts out the enemy from before the forward march of the soul He loves; the safe though isolated dwelling of Israel; the fertility of the soil and the generosity of the clouds; the blessedness of having Jehovah as the shield of help and the sword of excellency - all these features of the blessed life are delineated by the master-hand of one who dipped his brush in the colours mixed by his own experience.

What glimpses we get of the inner life of this noble man! All that he wrought on earth was the outcome of the secret abiding of his soul in God. God was his home, his help, his stay. He was nothing: God was all. And all that he accomplished on the earth was due to that Mighty One indwelling, fulfilling, and working out through him, as his organ and instrument, his own consummate plans.

Thus Moses drew his life-work to a close. Behind him, a long and glorious life, before, the ministry and worship of the heavenly sanctuary. Here, the shekinah; there, the unveiled face. Here, the tent and pilgrim march; there, the everlasting rest. Here, the promised land, beheld from afar, but not entered; there, the goodly land beyond Jordan entered and possessed. What though it was a wrench to pass away, with the crowning-stone not placed on the structure of his life; to depart and be with God was far better!

11

The Divine Summons

'Get thee out of thy country, and from thy kindred, and from thy father's house, unto the land that I will show thee: and I will make of thee a great nation, and I will bless thee, and make thy name great; and thou shalt be a blessing'
(Genesis 12:1, 2).

Whilst Abraham was living quietly in Ur, protesting against the idolatry of his times, with all its attendant evils, and according to tradition, suffering bitter persecution for conscience sake, 'The God of glory appeared unto him, and said, Get thee out of thy country, and from thy kindred, and come into the land which I shall show thee' (Acts 7:2, 3).

This was the first of those marvellous appearances which anticipated the Incarnation; and marked the successive stages of God's manifestation of Himself to men.

When this Divine appearance came we do not know; it may have been in the still and solemn night, or in the evening hour of meditation; or amid the duties of his position: but suddenly there shone from heaven a great light round about him, and a visible form appeared in the heart of the glory, and a voice spake the message of heaven in his ear. Not thus does God now appear to us; and yet it is certain that He still speaks in the silence of the waiting spirit, impressing His will, and saying, 'Get thee out.' Listen for that voice in the inner shrine of thine heart.

This same voice has often spoken since. It called Elijah from Thisbe, and Amos from Tekoa; Peter from his fishing nets, and Matthew from his toll-booth; Cromwell from his farm in Huntingdon, and Luther from his cloister at Erfurt. It ever sounds the perpetual summons of God, 'Come out from her, My people, that ye be not partakers of her sins, and that ye receive not of her plagues'; 'Come out from among them, and be ye separate, saith the Lord, and touch not the unclean thing.' Has it not come to you? Strange, if it has not. Yet, if it has, let nothing hinder your obedience; strike your tents, and follow where the God of glory beckons; and in that word *Come*, understand that He is moving on in front, and that if you would have His companionship, you must follow.

(1) This Call involved Hardship

He was a childless man. He had sufficient for the supply of his needs. He was deeply attached to those who were united to him by the close ties of a common nature. It was no small matter for him to break up his camp, to tear himself from his nearest and dearest, and to start for a land which, as yet, he did not know.

And so must it always be. The summons of God will ever involve a wrench from much that nature holds dear. We must be prepared to take up our cross daily if we would follow where He points the way. Each step of real advance in the Divine life will involve an altar on which some dear fragment of the self-life has been offered; or a cairn beneath which some cherished idol has been buried.

It is true that the blessedness which awaits us will more than compensate us for the sacrifices which we may have to make. And the prospect of the future may well allure us forward; but still, when it comes to the point, there is certain anguish as the last link is broken, the last farewell said, and the last look taken of the receding home of past happy years. And this is God's winnowing-fan, which clearly separates chaff and wheat. Many cannot endure a test so severe and searching in its demands. Like Pliable, they get out of the slough by the side nearest to their home. Like the young man, they go away sorrowful from the One to whom they had come with haste. Shall this be the case with you? Will you hear the call of God and shrink back from its cost? Count the cost clearly indeed; but, having done so, go forward in the name and by the strength of Him in whom all things are possible and easy and safe. And in doing so you will approve yourself worthy to stand with Christ in the regeneration.

Nothing is more clear than that, in these critical days, God is summoning the whole Church to a great advance, not only in knowledge, and in spiritual experience, but also in the evangelisation of the world. Blessed are they who are privileged to have a share in this sublime campaign!

(2) But the Call was eminently wise

It was for *Abraham himself*. Nothing strengthens us so much as isolation and transplantation. Let a young man emigrate, or be put into a responsible position; let him be thrown on his own resources - and he will develop powers of which there would have been no trace, if he had always lived at home, dependent on others, and surrounded by luxury. Under the wholesome demand his soul will put forth all her native vigour.

But what is true of the natural qualities of the soul is pre-eminently true of faith. So long as we are quietly at rest amid favourable and undisturbed surroundings, faith sleeps as an undeveloped sinew within us; a thread, a germ, an idea. But when we are pushed out from all these surroundings, with nothing but God to look to, then faith grows suddenly into a cable, a monarch oak, a master-principle of the life.

As long as the bird lingers by the nest, it will not know the luxury of flight. As long as the trembling boy holds to the bank, or toes the bottom, he will not learn the ecstasy of battling with the ocean wave. As long as men cling to the material, they cannot appreciate the reality of the promises of God. Abram could never have become Abraham, the father of the faithful, the mighty exemplar of faith, if he had always lived in Ur. No; he must quit his happy home, and journey forth into the untried and unknown, that faith may rise up to all its glorious proportions in his soul.

It may not be necessary for us to withdraw from home and friends; but we shall have to withdraw our heart's deepest dependence from all earthly props and supports, if ever we are to learn what it is to trust simply and absolutely on the eternal God. It may be that He is breaking away just now the shores on which we have been leaning, that the ship may glide down upon the ocean wave.

It was wise *for the world's sake*. On this one man rested the hope for the future of the world. Had he remained in Ur, it is impossible to say whether he would have continued true; or whether he might not have been seriously infected by the idolatry around. Or, even if he had been enabled to resist the adverse influences, his family, and, above all, his children, might have failed beneath the terrible ordeal. Was it not, therefore, wise for the world's sake, and for the sake of the Divine purposes, that he should be taken right away from his home and early associations, to find a fresh religious starting-point for the race, on new soil, and under new conditions?

Was it not thus that, in days of abounding vice and superstition, God led the Pilgrim Fathers to cross the seas, and found a new world, on the inhospitable shores of New England? And has it not been the plan of the Divine government in all ages? It is impossible to move our times, so long as we live beneath their spell; but when once we have risen up, and gone, at the call of God, outside their pale, we are able to react on them with an irresistible power. Archimedes vaunted that he could lift the world, if only he could obtain, outside of it, a pivot on which to rest his lever. Do not be surprised then, if God calls you out to be a people to Himself, that by you He may react with blessed power on the great world of men.

Sometimes, indeed, He bids us stay where we are, to glorify Him there. But oftenest He bids us leave unhallowed companionships, irreligious associations, evil fellowships and partnerships, and at great cost to get ourselves away into the isolation of a land which He promises to reveal.

(3) This Call was accompanied by Promise

God's commands are not always accompanied by reasons, but always by promises, expressed or understood. To give reasons would excite discussion; but to give a promise shows that the reason, though hidden, is all-sufficient. We can understand the promise, though the reason might baffle and confuse us. The reason is intellectual, metaphysical, spiritual; but a promise is practical, positive, literal. As a shell encloses a kernel, so do the Divine commands hide promises in their heart. If this is the command: 'Believe on the Lord Jesus Christ'; this is the promise: 'And thou shalt be saved'. If this is the command: 'Sell that thou hast and give to the poor'; this is the promise: 'Thou shalt have treasure in heaven'. If this is the command: 'Leave father and mother, houses and lands'; this is the promise: 'Thou shalt have a hundredfold here, and everlasting life beyond'. If this is the command: 'Be ye separate'; this is the promise: 'I will receive you and be a Father unto you'. So in this case: 'Though thou art childless, I will make of thee a great nation: though thou art the youngest son, I will bless thee, and make thy name great: though thou art to be torn from thine own family, in thee shall all the nations of the earth be blessed.' And each of those promises has been literally fulfilled.

It may seem that the hardships involved in the summons to exile are too great to be borne; yet study well the promise which is attached. And as the 'City which hath foundations' looms on the view, it will dwarf the proportions of the Ur in which you have been content to spend your days; and you will rise to be gone. Sometimes, therefore, it seems easier not to dwell on the sacrifice involved, but on the contents of the Divine and gracious promise. Bid people take; and they will give up of themselves. Let men find in Jesus the living water, and, like the woman of Samaria, they will leave their water-pots. Fire the hearts of the young with all the beauty and blessedness of the service of Jesus; and they will not find it so hard to leave nets, and fishing-boats, and friends, to forsake all and follow Him. 'When it pleased God to reveal His Son in me... immediately I conferred not with flesh and blood'.

St Francis de Sales used to say, 'When the house is on fire, men are ready to throw everything out of the window; and when the heart is full of God's true love, men are sure to count all else but worthless.'

(4) This Call teaches us the Meaning of Election

Everywhere we find beings and things more loftily endowed than others of the same kind. This is markedly evident in the religious sphere. And there is at first a jarring wonder at the apparent inequality of the Divine arrangements; until we understand that the superior endowment of the few is intended to enable them the better to help and bless the rest. 'I will bless thee, and thou shalt be a blessing.'

A great thinker feels that his end is approaching; he has made grand discoveries, but he has not as yet given them to the world. He selects one of his most promising pupils, and carefully indoctrinates him with his system; he is very severe on any inaccuracies and mistakes; he is very careful to give line on line. Why does he take all this care? For the sake of the young man? Not exclusively for the pupil's benefit; but that he may be able to give to the world those thoughts which his dying master has confided to his care. The young disciple is blessed that he may pass the blessings on to others.

Is not this a glimpse into the intention of God, in selecting Abraham, and in him the whole family of Israel? It was not so much with a view to their personal salvation, though that was included; but that they might pass on the holy teachings and oracles with which they were entrusted. It would have been worse than useless to have given such jewels directly to mankind. As well put a gorgeous banquet before a hungry babe. To say the least, there was no language ready in which to enshrine the sacred thoughts of God. The genius of truth required that the minds of men should be prepared to apprehend its sacred lessons. It was needful that definitions and methods of expression should be first well learnt by the people, who, when they had learnt them, might become the teachers of mankind.

The deep question is, whether election has not much more to do with our ministry than with our personal salvation. It brings less of rest, and peace, and joy, than it does of anguish, bitterness, and sorrow of heart. There is no need to envy God's elect ones. They are the exiles, the cross-bearers, the martyrs amongst men; but careless of themselves, they are all the while learning God's deepest lessons, away from the ordinary haunts of men; and they return to them presently with discoveries that pass all human thought, and are invaluable for human life.

(5) This Call gives the Key to Abraham's Life

It rang a clarion note at the very outset, which continued to vibrate through all his after-history. The key to Abraham's life is the word 'Separation'. He was from first to last a *separated man*. Separated from his fatherland and kinsfolk; separated from Lot; separated, as a pilgrim and stranger, from the people of the land; separated from his own methods of securing a fulfilment of the promises of God; separated from the rest of mankind by special sorrows, which brought him into closer fellowship with God than has ever been reached by man; separated to high and lofty fellowship in thoughts and plans, which God could not hide from him.

But it was the Separation of Faith

There is a form of separation known amongst men, in which the lonely soul goes apart, to secure uninterrupted leisure for devotion; spending the slow-passing hours in vigil, fasting and prayer; hoping to win salvation as the guerdon of its austerities. This is not the separation to which God called Abraham, or to which we are summoned.

Abraham's separation is not like that of those who wish to be saved; but rather that of those who are saved. Not towards the Cross, but from it. Not to merit anything, but, because the heart has seen the Vision of God, and cannot now content itself with the things that once fascinated and entranced it; so that leaving them behind, it reaches out its hands in eager longing for eternal realities, and thus is led gradually and insensibly out and away from the seen to the unseen, and from the temporal to the eternal.

May such separation be ours! May we catch the Divine Call, irradiated by the Divine Promise! And as we hear of that fair land, of that glorious city, of those Divine delights which await us, may we leave and relinquish those lesser and injurious things which have held us too long, spoiling our peace, and sapping our power; and, striking our tents, obey our God's behest, though it may lead us whither we know not!

12

Arrest and Defeat
(Joshua 8:1, 2)

*'"Now, Christians, hold your own - the land before ye
Is open - win your way, and take your rest."
So sounds our war-note; but our path of glory
By many a cloud is darkened and unblest.'*

(Keble)

The conquest of Canaan occupied seven years, and during the whole of that time Israel lost but one battle; indeed, the six-and-thirty men smitten in the headlong flight before the men of Ai seem to have been the only loss which their hosts sustained. The story of this defeat is told with great minuteness; because it involved lessons of the greatest moment to Israel, and of incalculable value to ourselves.

The experience of defeat is far too common to the majority of Christians. They are constantly turning their backs before their enemies. They are defeated by indwelling sin and the assaults of Satan, and by the mighty evils which they assail in the name of God. But instead of taking their defeats to heart, they become inured to them. For the time they are filled with mortification and chagrin; but the impression soon wears away. They do not lie on their faces before God, eager to discover the cause of failure, to deal with it, and to advance from the scene of defeat to wider and more permanent success. If we but carefully investigated the causes of our defeats, they would be only second to victories in their blessed results on our characters and lives.

There were three causes for this defeat.

(1) They were Self-confident because Ai was small

Jericho was a heap of smouldering ruins. Man and woman, both young and old, and ox, and sheep, and ass, all had been utterly destroyed with the edge of the sword. The only relics were - the silver and gold and vessels of brass and iron, which had been placed among the precious stores of the Tabernacle; the woman Rahab, her people and her property; and a certain Babylonish garment, some silver shekels, and a wedge of gold, of which we shall hear again.

Fearing no attack from the rear, Joshua at once set his face towards the interior of the country, and chose a deep gorge or ravine, which lay a little towards the north, as the passageway for his army. Eight miles from its opening on the Jordan valley this ravine met another, 'in a wild entanglement of hill and valley', and near the junction of the two stood the little town of Ai, with a population of twelve thousand persons. The proportion of fighting men has been calculated at about two thousand; but the situation was strong and commanded the pass, so that Joshua had no alternative but to mete out to it the same terrible fate as that with which he had visited Jericho.

Speaking after the manner of men, there was considerable force in the report of the spies sent up the valley to reconnoitre. The place was much smaller than Jericho, and would apparently require much less expenditure of time and strength for its capture. Jericho may have needed the entire host; but for Ai, some three thousand men would surely suffice. 'Make not all the people to toil thither; for they (i.e. the men of Ai) are but few'.

But this recommendation went on the supposition that Jericho had been overthrown by the attack of the hosts of Israel; whereas in point of fact they had had singularly little to do with it. They had walked around it and shouted - that was all. It had been taken by their great Captain and Leader, and by Him given into their hands. The silence that reigned over its site was no criterion of their might, but of his. To speak as they did was to ignore the real facts of the case, and to argue as though the victory were due to some inherent qualities in themselves; with the inference that because they had conquered at Jericho they must therefore necessarily conquer at Ai.

There is no experience in the Christian life so full of peril as the hour when we are flushed with recent victory. Then comes the temptation to sacrifice to our net, and burn incense to our drag. We magnify our part in the conflict till it fills the whole range of vision. We boast to ourselves that we have gotten the land in possession by our own sword, and that our own arm has saved us. Counting from our great triumph at Jericho, we despise such a small obstacle as Ai. Surely, we argue, if we have carried the one, we shall easily prevail at the other! And so it frequently happens that a great success in public is followed by a fall in private; that those who had swept all before them in the pulpit or on the platform are overcome by some miserable appetite, or by petulance in the home; and the bitter regret of that sin wipes out all the glad exhilaration of the hour of victory. We never so need to observe the injunction to 'watch and pray' as when the foe is flying before us. When the mighty convocation breaks up, its convictions having been turned by our single voice - as in the story of Elijah - and as the people are departing to their homes, and the bodies of the priests of Baal choke the Kishon, we must be careful to go up to the top of Carmel, where we had girded ourselves for the conflict, and, bowing to the earth, put our face between our knees in prayer.

Had Joshua acted thus he would never have been induced by the word of the spies to reason on mere military grounds; he would never have presumed on the insignificance of the little town; and he would never have had the anguish of seeing his panic-stricken soldiers come rushing down the rugged pass, or sheltering in the stone-quarries on either hand, whilst the men of Ai, in full pursuit, were cutting down the hindmost and least nimble.

There is nothing small in Christian life - nothing so small that we can combat it in our own strength. Apart from God the smallest temptations will be more than a match for us. So weak are we that occasions of sin, which are perfectly contemptible in themselves, will overthrow our most confident resolutions. The victories which we have won in fellowship with God have imparted no inherent might to us; we are as weak as ever; and directly we are brought into collision with the least of our enemies, apart from Him, we shall inevitably go down before the shock. The faith, watchfulness, and fellowship with God, which availed before Jericho, can alone serve as the key to Ai.

(2) They Failed to Wait on God

An accursed thing in their midst broke the link of fellowship between them and the hosts that served beneath the celestial Warrior who had appeared to Joshua. And though it must have been a severe sorrow to Jehovah to inflict sorrow on His people, yet for their sake, and for the sake of His holy name, the sin must be judged and put away. Joshua pleaded, 'What wilt Thou do for Thy great Name?' But it was for that very reason that the defeat had been permitted.

There is not the least doubt that if Joshua had been in

113

abiding fellowship with God, the Spirit of God would have indicated the presence of evil in the host; so that Achan and his sin would have been discovered and judged before the march to Ai. It was so in an analogous case in the Acts of the Apostles. What Achan was to Israel, that Ananias and his wife were to the early Church. The fifth chapter of the Acts would have recorded some great defeat or crushing disaster, if it had not contained the story of the discernment on the part of the apostle Peter, and by the Holy Ghost, of the accursed thing to which the guilty pair were privy.

If we may dare to imagine what would have been the consequence in the primitive Church had that root of evil been left unextirpated, we should be obliged not only to wipe out the record of the signs and wonders wrought among the people, of the unity of the disciples, and of the burst doors of the prison; but we should have to interpolate an account of how the hosts of God, in diminished numbers, gave back before the fury of their adversaries; of how Peter lay with his face in the dust of the Temple courts; of how panic and dismay filled the hearts of leaders and led; and of how the name of the Lord Jesus was blasphemed and His character traduced. But none of these things befell, because the Spirit of God was able to utter His unhindered testimony.

Very important is it for us to heed the apostle's warning, 'if we discerned ourselves we should not be judged'. God sees the little rift in the lute; the spot of decay in the fruit; the ulcer in the flesh, threatening to eat away its vitality. These may not be realised by us; but He knows how inevitably they must lead to defeat. Nor is He slow to warn us of them. Yet of what use is it for Him to speak to deaf ears; or to those who are self-confident in their own wisdom; or who pride themselves on victories which were wholly His gift? Amid the gaiety of the revel, we do not see the handwriting on the wall; amid the unanimous advice of the false prophets we do not inquire for the one voice that may speak evil of our plans; amid the radiant sunlight of the morning, in which the dancing wavelets flash, we do not care to see the falling glass, or be guided by the dark prognostications of the weather-beaten sailor. Probably there is no single temptation which has not to claim permission of God before it touches us. He who permits it prays for us, raising His voice in lonely vigil whilst we sleep, anticipating the attack by ambushes of intercession. Yea, not content with this, He warns us not once nor twice; He even touches us with fingers that would thrill us were we not insensible, steeped in spiritual lethargy.

Where God's children, like Joshua, are oblivious to the warning voices, which speak in ever fainter tones as they are disregarded, God is compelled to let them take their course until some terrible disaster flings them on their faces to the ground. Ah, if Joshua had only prostrated himself amid the shoutings of victory over Jericho, there would have been no need for him to prostrate himself amid the outcry of a panic-stricken host! If he had only sought counsel of God before he sent the spies up the pass, there would have been no need to ask what he should do to repair his defeat. The iron pruning-knife of trouble has to do for many of us, roughly and hurtfully, what the silver pruning-knife of the Word of God might have effected.

Before ever we make some new advance, although the point of attack be but an Ai, it is our duty, as it is our best policy, to get back to Gilgal. Joshua does not seem to have returned there after the fall of Jericho. We ought to seclude

115

ourselves in spiritual converse with our Almighty Confederate, asking if He has aught to say to us; entreating that He should reveal any evil thing that He may see in us, and mustering the tribes of our heart before his scrutiny, that the Achan lurking there may be brought to light before, instead of after, the fight.

(3) They had Committed a Trespass in the Devoted Thing

(a) Joshua was inclined to lay the charge of their failure on God. It seemed to him as if the Almighty had done ill by them in bringing them into the heart of such mighty difficulties. In his judgment, warped by the presence of disaster, it appeared as if it had been better for the camp to have remained on the other side of Jordan. The dreariest anticipations of defeat and destruction passed in spectral form before him. He spoke as one whom faith had deserted, the locks of his might shorn, and himself no longer a hero, but, like the Canaanites themselves, whose heart had melted as his did now. But, in point of fact, the blame lay not with God, who was engaged in conducting His people within reach of superlative blessedness, but wholly with themselves.

There are times in our lives when we are disposed to find fault with God. 'Why, Great Potter, hast Thou made me thus? Why was I ever taken out of my quiet home, or country parish, or happy niche of service, to be plunged into this sea of difficulties?' When we are smarting from some defeat, caused by the overpowering might or the clever strategy of the foe, we are prone to blame God; either that our nature was not stronger, or that He has brought us from the shelter of comparative obscurity, and placed us on the mountain slope where the storms expend their wildest fury. Alas! we forget that our Father brings us across the Jordan to give us larger experiences, to open before us vaster possibilities, to give us a better chance of acquiring His unsearchable riches. There is no task without sufficiency of grace; no foe without a sufficiency of victorious power; no trial without a sufficiency of resource by which, as in the old dream of the alchemist, the hardest, commonest metal may be transformed to gold.

The defeats that we incur in the Land of Promise are not necessary. They are due entirely to some failure in ourselves, and they cause grief to the immortal Lover of our souls. There is no reason for defeat in the Christian life; always, and everywhere we are meant to be more than conquerors. The course of the Christian warrior should be as the sun when he goeth forth in his strength, and in regular gradients drives his chariot from the eastern wave up the steep of heaven. Child of God, never lay the blame of your failure on God; seek for it within!

(b) One Israelite only had trespassed, and yet it is said, '*The children of Israel* committed a trespass in the devoted thing'. Not one of us stands alone; we cannot sin without insensibly affecting the spiritual condition of all our fellows. We cannot grow cold without lowering the temperature of all contiguous hearts. We cannot pass upward without lifting others. No asteroid revolves through space without affecting the position and speed of every member of its system. No grain lies upon the seashore without influencing all its companion grains. 'None of us liveth to himself, and none dieth to himself.' 'Whether one member suffereth, all the members suffer with it; or one member is honoured, all the members rejoice with it.'

If Israel had but realised how much the safety of the

117

whole depended on the obedience of each, every individual would have watched his brethren, as he watched himself, not for their sakes alone, but for his own; and did the members of Christian communities understand how vast an influence for weal or woe depends upon the choice, the decision, the action of any, there would be a fuller and more intelligent obedience to the reiterated injunctions of the New Testament - for the strong to bear the infirmities of the weak; for the loftiest to stoop to wash the feet of the lowliest; and for all to look not on their own things only, but also on the things of others. 'Looking carefully less any man fail of the grace of God.'

Should these words be read by any soul which is conscious of playing an Achan's part, let it take warning, and whilst it is called Today, confess, restore, and repent. Not only that it may escape an inevitable judgment; but that it may not bring disaster and defeat upon those with whom it associates, dragging the innocent down into the vortex of a common fate. The hands of Achan were stained with the blood of the thirty-six that perished in the flight to Shebarim.

(c) How careless we are of God's distinct prohibitions! Nothing could have been more clearly promulgated than the command to leave the spoils of Jericho untouched. The city and its contents were devoted to utter destruction, a specified number of articles only being preserved for Tabernacle use. This ordinance was probably intended to preserve the children of Israel from the temptation which must have accrued, had they glutted themselves with the spoils of the city. The abstinence tended to strengthen their character, and to educate their faith. But to Achan, the will of God was overborne by the lust of his eyes and the pride

118

of life. The strong tide of passion swept him over the barrier reared by the Divine word.

Let us not, however, judge him too hardly. He is not the last who has acted in distinct violation of Divine commands. The Bible is full of prohibitions against the love of the world, the love of dress, the love of money; against censoriousness, and pride, and unhallowed ambition; against the Babylonish garment and the wedge of gold: and yet thousands of Christian people live in complacent disobedience, as if God were one of themselves, or as if his words were unsubstantial as smoke. What wonder that the forces of his Israel meet with defeat, and that the old word is verified in individual experience and in the history of the church, 'Israel hath sinned; yea, they have even transgressed My covenant which I commanded them; yea, they have even taken of the devoted thing. Therefore they cannot stand before their enemies. I will not be with you any more, except ye destroy the devoted thing from among you.'

13

The Banquet

*'Thou preparest a table before me,
In the presence of mine enemies'*

(Psalm 23:5).

At first it seems difficult to catch the exact sequence of the Psalmist's thought, as he turns from the sheep-cotes to the festal-board. And yet the demands of the spiritual life so far transcend all earthly analogies, as to demand that more than one metaphor should be employed, one supplying what the other lacks, so that the true conception of our relationship to God may be complete.

Now it is of course very helpful to think of one's self as a sheep, and of Christ as a Shepherd; but there can be no fellowship between the dumb animals and their watchful keeper. The little child that comes from the shepherd's shieling to meet its father has more intimate fellowship with him, though it can hardly articulate its words, than the dumb creatures of his care.

The Psalmist, therefore, seems to say 'I am more than Jehovah's sheep; I am Jehovah's guest.' It is a mark of great intimacy to sit with a man at his table; in the East it is essentially so. It is not only a means of satisfying hunger, but of intimate and affectionate love. Hence the aggravation of the Psalmist's sorrow, as he said, 'He that breaketh bread with me is he that lifteth up his heel against me.' Nor was it possible for our Lord to give any more touching proof of His love for His wayward follower than to dip a sop and pass it to his hands. Here, then, arises before us a rich theme for meditation whilst we compare life to a seat at God's banquet table, eating the things which He has prepared.

We sit at the table of God's daily providence

Our Heavenly Father has a great family. He is weighted with the concerns of a universe. All sentient things depend upon His sustaining power. Not a seraph cleaves the air but what derives his power of obedience from his sovereign Lord; and not a mote of life floats in the sunbeam, flashing in the glad light, but it is dependent upon the light and life of the central Sun, before whom angels veil their faces.

And yet, amidst all the infinite variety of nature which God is supplying constantly, He is surely most attentive to the needs of those who, in an especial sense, call Him 'Our Father'. We are His pensioners; nay, better - we are His children! All the stores of His divine provision must fail before He can suffer us to want. He may sometimes keep us waiting until His hour has struck; but just as He will never be one moment too soon, so He will not be a moment too late. He will cause a widow woman to sustain us with the barrel of meal, which, however often scraped, will yield a fresh supply. He will rain bread from heaven so that man may eat angels' food. He will multiply the slender store of the boy's wallet, so that present need may be met, and stores accumulated for the future.

On a recent Sunday evening, a sick member of a congregation, debarred from attending her customary place of worship, entrusted to the hand of the minister a two-shilling piece, which he was to hand to a poor widow known to them both. It so happened that he encountered her slowly making her way to the church, and at once handed

121

to her the coin. But he was hardly prepared for the immediate response: 'I did not think that He would have sent it so soon.' On further inquiry he discovered that she had placed her last coin that day in the collection, and was entirely dependent upon such answer as her Heavenly Father might send to her trustful prayer that He would provide for her next meal. Evidently she had been accustomed to close dealings with God, and had learned that His deliverance is timed to arrive 'when the morning breaks' - the morning of direst need; the hour when pride and self-sufficiency have expired; but when faith and hope stand still expectant at the portals of the soul looking out for the deliverance, which cannot be long delayed.

I never shall forget the story of an old man, discovered sitting in one of the seats of York Minster, within a short period of closing time, and who had been sitting there since the early morning, waiting. He had come to the city to find his daughter; but, having missed her, had found himself without friends or food, and with his last coin spent. Not knowing whither to turn, he had found his way into the splendid Minster, and had sat there the livelong day; because, as he said, he thought the likeliest place to find his Father's table was in his Father's house. Need I add that his need was fully satisfied.

God's children seem to think that they are no better off than men of the world. And, according to their faith, so it is done unto them. If we do not exercise faith, and claim God's provisions, ought we to be surprised when we do not receive them? If, on the other hand, we would dare to put our finger upon His promises, which bind Him to meet His children's need, though the young lions lack and suffer hunger, we should find that our God would be equal to all our emergencies, and that not one good thing would fail of all His promises. When men indicate certain cases in which God's children have pined to death, it is always wise to inquire whether they were living in believing fellowship with Him, and whether they had claimed the fulfilment of His specific pledges. It is very unbecoming, to say the least, that God's children should be as fretful about their daily bread, supposing they are using all lawful methods to obtain it, as the children of men. Was it not with a tone of reproach that our Lord said, 'After all these things do the Gentiles seek'? And what could be more reassuring than His own words, backed by the experience of His own life? - 'Your Heavenly Father knoweth that ye have need of all these things.'

What would you say if, when school-time came tomorrow morning, your little boy - before he started with unwilling feet to the school - entered your larder, and busied himself in examining its contents, with especial reference to your provision for dinner? Would he not legitimately incur your displeasure? Would you not say? - 'Be off to school, and leave me to care whilst you are gone!' Would you not rebuke him for his want of simple trust? Oh that we might learn lessons from our babes, and believe that life is one long residence in one of the mansions of our Father's home; and that the time can never come when the table is quite bare, and when there is nothing for our need! He may suffer you to hunger, because there are some devils which will only go forth by prayer and fasting; but, sooner or later, His angel will touch you, saying, 'Arise, and eat': and on the desert floor you will find, spread by angel-hands, a banquet, though it be nothing more than a cruse of water at your head, and cakes bakened on the hot stones of the wilderness, for your repast.

God also prepares the table of spiritual refreshment

Can we ever forget that episode - among the most charming incidents in the forty days - in which, as the weary fishers emerged with empty boats from a long, toilsome night, they found a banquet spread for them, by the tender thoughtfulness of their Lord, upon the strand of the lake? As soon as they touched land they saw a fire of coals, and fish laid thereon, and bread. And is not this an emblem of our Lord's perpetual treatment of His children? Tired, disappointed with fruitless toils, agitated by conflicting hopes and fears, we often pull to the shore trodden by His blessed feet; nor do we ever approach Him without finding that He has anticipated our spiritual requirements, and that 'His flesh is meat indeed, and His blood drink indeed'.

Writing to the Corinthian Christians, the apostle Paul said that, inasmuch as Christ had been slain as our Passover Lamb, we must imitate the children of Israel, who, with closed doors and girded loins and sandalled feet, stood around the table eating of the flesh of the lamb, whose blood on the exterior of their houses demanded their deliverance. 'Christ our Passover is sacrificed for us; let us therefore keep the feast.' The life of the Church, between the first and second advents, is symbolised by the feast on that memorable night. With joy in our voices and triumph in our mien, we stand around the table where Christ's flesh is the nourishment of all true hearts, straining our ear for the first clarion notes which will tell that the time of our exodus has come. Christian people are very much too thoughtless of the necessity of feeding off God's table for the nourishment of spiritual life. There is plenty of work being done; much attendance at conferences and special missions; diligent reading of religious books; but there is a great and fatal lack of the holy meditation upon the person, the words and the work of the Lord Jesus Christ.

Will each reader of these lines stay here for a moment, and ask if he knows anything of the interior life of meditation, which is ever deriving fresh sustenance from a consideration of the Lord.

It was only the other day that I was rebuked by the habit of St Francis de Sales of whom it is said, 'The first point of his rule was early rising, which he faithfully practised to the last day of his life, and often recommended to others. He was the first on foot at his palace, and began his prayers and meditation between four and five o'clock in the morning, and never spent less at them than an hour. He often did this with his memoranda in his hand, so as to recall past graces and thus rekindle the flame. Nor did it seem as if any hour passed in his crowded and stirring life, without by some direct act refreshing his soul by communion with God'.

And, in addition to this daily practice, he set apart one or two weeks in every year, that he might quietly meditate more patiently upon the great mysteries of redemption. This is what he said: 'One must, by constant meditation on the great mysteries of incarnation and the redemption, plunge one's self more and more in the love of God, which is the greatest grace of one's life. I will occupy myself more and more with our Lord: with His earthly and divine life; with His hidden suffering and glorious life. May my own be hidden in God in Jesus Christ!'

We may specially apply these words also to the table of the Lord's Supper
This is emphatically a table which God has prepared; which not only perpetuates the memory of the night in which our

Lord was betrayed, but which enables us to raise our wandering thoughts, and to fix them on Him where He is now seated. There is no mystic change made in the bread or in the wine. The bread remains bread and the wine wine to the end of the simple feast; and yet, at the moment of partaking of these elements, the pious heart does realise that, by its faith and holy thought, a distinct blessing is communicated to its invigoration and comfort. It is well, of course, at that solemn moment to recall the agony and bloody sweat, the cross and passion, the precious death and burial; but it is equally incumbent to look through the azure depths and to follow the Master through their parted folds, so as to feed upon His resurrection life and to participate in the perpetual Easter-tide of His existence.

It is very helpful, where possible, to communicate at least once each week; that we may clearly learn to lift all life to the level of the Lord's table, to be at every meal as at a sacrament, and to use all the emblems of nature as means of holy fellowship with Him. How can we enough thank God that in this sense also He has prepared a table before us?

There is much comfort in the three words 'prepared for me'; because it would seem to indicate the *anticipatory care of God*. He does not allow us to be taken by surprise. He does not let His children ask for anything the need of which He has not foreseen. Just as He has prepared beforehand the good works in which we are to walk, so has He prepared beforehand the food by which His workers shall be nourished. All our life's path is lined by cairns beneath which our Forerunner has placed the victuals which we shall require. 'Thou preventest me with the blessings of Thy goodness.' The table is spread before the hunger comes. The spring is bubbling in the shade before mother and child sink fainting on the sand.

The Angel of the Lord's host has not only taken possession of the hostile country, but has provided of the old corn of the land. God provisions His castles before they are besieged. 'Thou *preparest* before me a table.'

That is a very significant addition - *in the presence of mine enemies*. We surely are to understand by it that all around us may stand our opponents - pledged to do us harm; to cut off our supplies; to starve us out. See that ring of hostile faces, darting fierce glances and chafing to rush upon the beleaguered soul! But they cannot cut off the supplies that come hourly from above. They cannot hinder the angel ministers who spread the table and heap it up, and then form themselves into an inner ring of defence. They may gnash their teeth at the vanity and futility of their rage; but when God elects to feed a soul, fed that soul shall be, though all hell attempt to say it nay! Many a time in David's life he ate his food in quietness and confidence, whilst Saul's hostile bands swept down the valleys, and searched the caves to find him. As it was with David, so it has been often since.

Yes, soul, God bids thee feast; 'eat, O beloved, yea, eat and drink abundantly'. The King doth bring thee into His banqueting house, and His banner over thee is love. Thou shalt eat of the hidden manna and drink of the secret spring which bubbles up in the beleaguered city, enabling it to defy the encircling lines of its foes. Nor is the time far distant when we shall sit with Christ in His kingdom; and, as the far-travelled footsore brethren of Joseph ate with the prince who once lay in the pit, so shall we sit down at the prepared table of the marriage supper, and Christ will gird Himself and come forth to serve us, and the festivities of an eternity, which shall never know penury or want, shall obliterate the memory of the sorrows of time.

14

The Secret of Guidance

Many children of God are so deeply exercised on the matter of guidance that it may be helpful to give a few suggestions as to knowing the way in which our Father would have us walk, and the work He would have us do. The importance of the subject cannot be exaggerated; so much of our power and peace consists in knowing where God would have us be, and in being just there.

The manna only falls where the cloudy pillar broods; but it is certain to be found on the sands, which a few hours ago were glistening in the flashing light of the heavenly fire, and are now shadowed by the fleecy canopy of cloud. If we are precisely where our heavenly Father would have us to be, we are perfectly sure that He will provide food and raiment, and everything beside. When He sends His servants to Cherith, He will make even the ravens to bring them food.

How much of our Christian work has been abortive, because we have persisted in initiating it for ourselves, instead of ascertaining what God was doing, and where He required our presence. We dream bright dreams of success. We try and command it. We call to our aid all kinds of expedients, questionable or otherwise. And at last we turn back, disheartened and ashamed, like children who are torn and scratched by the brambles, and soiled by the quagmire. None of this had come about, if only we had been, from the first, under God's unerring guidance. He might test us, but He could not allow us to mistake.

Naturally, the child of God, longing to know his Father's will, turns to the sacred Book, and refreshes his confidence by noticing how in all ages God has guided those who dared to trust Him up to the very hilt, but who, at the time, must have been as perplexed as we are often now. We know how Abraham left kindred and country, and started, with no other guide than God, across the trackless desert to a land which he knew not. We know how for forty years the Israelites were led through the peninsula of Sinai, with its labyrinths of red sandstone and its wastes of sand. We know how Joshua, in entering the Land of Promise, was able to cope with the difficulties of an unknown region, and to overcome great and warlike nations, because he looked to the Captain of the Lord's host, who ever leads to victory. We know how, in the early Church, the Apostles were enabled to thread their way through the most difficult questions, and to solve the most perplexing problems; laying down principles which will guide the Church to the end of time; and this because it was revealed to them as to what they should do and say, by the Holy Spirit.

The promises for guidance are unmistakable, Psalm 32:8: 'I will instruct thee and teach thee in the way which thou shalt go.' This is God's distinct assurance to those whose transgressions are forgiven, and whose sins are covered, and who are more quick to notice the least symptom of His will, than horse or mule to feel the bit.

Proverbs 3:6: 'In all thy ways acknowledge Him, and He shall direct (or make plain) thy paths.' A sure word, on which we may rest; if only we fulfil the previous conditions of trusting with all our heart and of not leaning to our own understanding.

Isaiah 58:11: 'The Lord shall guide thee continually.'

It is impossible to think that He could guide us at all, if He did not guide us always. For the greatest events of life, like the huge rocking-stones in the west of England, revolve on the smallest points. A pebble may alter the flow of a stream. The growth of a grain of mustard seed may determine the rainfall of a continent. Thus we are bidden to look for a Guidance which shall embrace the whole of life in all its myriad necessities.

John 8:12: 'I am the light of the world; he that followeth Me shall not walk in darkness, but shall have the light of life.' The reference here seems to be to the wilderness wanderings; and the Master promises to be to all faithful souls, in their pilgrimage to the City of God, what the cloudy pillar was to the children of Israel on their march to the Land of Promise.

These are but specimens. The vault of Scripture is inlaid with thousands such, that glisten in their measure as the stars which guide the wanderer across the deep. Well may the prophet sum up the heritage of the servants of the Lord by saying of the Holy City, 'All thy children shall be taught of the Lord, and great shall be the peace of thy children.'

And yet it may appear to some tried and timid hearts as if every one mentioned in the Word of God was helped, but they are left without help. They seem to have stood before perplexing problems, face to face with life's mysteries, eagerly longing to know what to do, but no angel has come to tell them, and no iron gate has opened to them in the prison-house of circumstances.

Some lay the blame on their own stupidity. Their minds are blunt and dull. They cannot catch God's meaning, which would be clear to others. They are so nervous of doing wrong, that they cannot learn clearly what is right.

'Who is blind, but my servant? or deaf, as my messenger that I sent? Who is blind as he that is perfect, and blind as the Lord's servant?' Yet, how do we treat our children? One child is so bright-witted and so keen that a little hint is enough to indicate the way; another was born dull: it cannot take in your meaning quickly. Do you only let the clever one know what you want? Will you not take the other upon your knee and make clear to it the directions which baffle it? Does not the distress of the tiny nursling, who longs to know that it may immediately obey, weave an almost stronger bond than that which binds you to the rest? Oh! weary, perplexed and stupid children, believe in the great love of God, and cast yourselves upon it, sure that He will come down to your ignorance, and suit Himself to your needs, and will take 'the lambs in His arms, and carry them in His bosom, and *gently lead* those that are with young'.

There are certain practical directions which we must attend to in order that we may be led into the mind of the Lord.

(1) Our Motives must be Pure

'When thine eye is single, thy whole body is also full of light' (Luke 11:34). You have been much in darkness lately, and perhaps this passage will point the reason. Your eye has not been single. There has been some obliquity of vision. A spiritual squint. And this has hindered you from discerning indications of God's will, which otherwise had been as clear as noonday.

We must be very careful in judging our motives: searching them as the detectives at the doors of the House of Commons search each stranger who enters. When, by the grace of God, we have been delivered from grosser forms

131

of sin, we are still liable to the subtle working of self in our holiest and loveliest hours. It poisons our motives. It breathes decay on our fairest fruit-bearing. It whispers seductive flatteries into our pleased ears. It turns the spirit from its holy purpose, as the masses of iron on ocean steamers deflect the needle of the compass from the pole.

So long as there is some thought of personal advantage, some idea of acquiring the praise and commendation of men, some aim at self-aggrandisement, it will be simply impossible to find out God's purpose concerning us. The door must be resolutely shut against all this, if we would hear the still small voice. All cross-lights must be excluded, if we would see the Urim and Thummim stone brighten with God's 'Yes' or darken with his 'No'.

Ask the Holy Spirit to give you the single eye, and to inspire in your heart one aim alone; that which animated our Lord, and enabled Him to cry, as He reviewed His life, 'I have glorified Thee on the earth.' Let this be the watchword of our lives, 'Glory to God in the highest.' Then our 'whole body shall be full of light, having no part dark, as when the bright shining of a candle doth give light'.

(2) Our Will must be Surrendered

'My judgment is just; because I seek not Mine own will, but the will of the Father which hath sent Me' (John 5:30). This was the secret, which Jesus not only practised, but taught. In one form or another He was constantly insisting on a surrendered will, as the key to perfect knowledge, 'If any man will do His will, he shall know.'

There is all the difference between a will which is extinguished and one which is surrendered. God does not demand that our wills should be crushed out, like the

132

sinews of a fakir's unused arm. He only asks that they should say 'Yes' to Him. Pliant to Him as the willow twig to the practised hand.

Many a time, as the steamer has neared the quay, have I watched the little lad take his place beneath the poop, with eye and ear fixed on the captain, and waiting to shout each word he utters to the grimy engineers below; and often have I longed that my will should repeat as accurately, and as promptly, the words and will of God, that all the lower nature might obey.

It is for the lack of this subordination that we so often miss the guidance we seek. There is a secret controversy between our will and God's. And we shall never be right till we have let Him take, and break, and make. Oh! do seek for that. If you cannot give, let Him take. If you are not willing, confess that you are willing to be made willing. Hand yourself over to Him to work in you, to will and to do of His own good pleasure. We must be as plastic clay, ready to take any shape that the great Potter may choose, so shall we be able to detect His guidance.

(3) We must seek Information for our Mind

This is certainly the next step. God has given us these wonderful faculties of brain power, and He will not ignore them. In the days of the Reformation He did not destroy the Roman Catholic churches or pulpits; He did better, He preached in them. And in grace He does not cancel the action of any of His marvellous bestowments, but He uses them for the communication of His purposes and thoughts.

It is of the greatest importance, then, that we should feed our minds with facts; with reliable information; with the results of human experience, and above all with the teachings of the Word of God. It is matter for the utmost admiration to notice how full the Bible is of biography and history: so that there is hardly a single crisis in our lives that may not be matched from those wondrous pages. There is no book like the Bible for casting a light on the dark landings of human life.

We have no need or right to run hither and thither to ask our friends what we ought to do; but there is no harm in our taking pains to gather all reliable information, on which the flame of holy thought and consecrated purpose may feed and grow strong. It is for us ultimately to decide as God shall teach us, but His voice may come to us through the voice of sanctified common sense, acting on the materials we have collected. Of course at times God may bid us act against our reason; but these are very exceptional; and then our duty will be so clear that there can be no mistake. But for the most part God will speak in the results of deliberate consideration, weighing and balancing the *pros* and *cons*.

When Peter was shut up in prison, and could not possibly extricate himself, an angel was sent to do for him what he could not do for himself; but when they had passed through a street or two of the city, the angel left him to consider the matter for himself. Thus God treats us still. He will dictate a miraculous course by miraculous methods. But when the ordinary light of reason is adequate to the task, He will leave us to act as occasion may serve.

(4) We must be much in Prayer for Guidance
The Psalms are full of earnest pleadings for clear direction: 'Show me Thy way, O Lord, lead me in a plain path, because of mine enemies.' It is the law of our Father's house that His children shall ask for what they want. 'If any

134

man lack wisdom, let him ask of God, who giveth to all men liberally, and upbraideth not.'

In a time of change and crisis, we need to be much in prayer, not only on our knees, but in that sweet form of inward prayer, in which the spirit is constantly offering itself up to God, asking to be shown His will; soliciting that it may be impressed upon its surface, as the heavenly bodies photograph themselves on prepared paper. Wrapt in prayer like this the trustful believer may tread the deck of the ocean steamer night after night, sure that He who points the stars their courses will not fail to direct the soul which has no other aim than to do His will.

One good form of prayer at such a juncture is to ask that doors may be shut, that the way may be closed, and that all enterprises which are not according to God's will may be arrested at their very beginning. Put the matter absolutely into God's hands from the outset, and he will not fail to shatter the project and defeat the aim which is not according to His holy will.

(5) We must wait the gradual Unfolding of God's Plan in Providence

God's impressions within and His word without are always corroborated by His Providence around, and we should quietly wait until these three focus into one point.

Sometimes it looks as if we are bound to act. Everyone says we must do something; and indeed things seem to have reached so desperate a pitch that we must. Behind are the Egyptians; right and left are inaccessible precipices; before is the sea. It is not easy at such times to stand still and see the salvation of God; but we must. When Saul compelled himself, and offered sacrifice, because he thought that Samuel was too late in coming, he made the great mistake of his life.

God may delay to come in the guise of His Providence. There was delay ere Sennacherib's host lay like withered leaves around the Holy City. There was delay ere Jesus came walking on the sea in the early dawn, or hastened to raise Lazarus. There was delay ere the angel sped to Peter's side on the night before his expected martyrdom. He stays long enough to test patience of faith, but not a moment behind the extreme hour of need. 'The vision is yet for an appointed time, but at the end it shall speak, and shall not lie; though it tarry, wait for it; because it will surely come; it will not tarry.'

It is very remarkable how God guides us by circumstances. At one moment the way may seem utterly blocked, and then shortly afterwards some trivial incident occurs, which might not seem much to others, but which to the keen eye of faith speaks volumes. Sometimes these signs are repeated in different ways in answer to prayer. They are not haphazard results of chance, but the opening-up of circumstances in the direction in which we should walk. And they begin to multiply, as we advance towards our goal, just as lights do as we near a populous town, when darting through the land by night express.

Sometimes men sigh for an angel to come to point them their way: that simply indicates that as yet the time has not come for them to move. If you do not know what you ought to do, stand still until you do. And when the time comes for action, circumstances, like glow-worms, will sparkle along your path; and you will become so sure that you are right, when God's three witnesses concur, that you could not be surer though an angel beckoned you on.

The circumstances of our daily life are to us an infallible

indication of God's will, when they concur with the inward promptings of the Spirit and with the Word of God. So long as they are stationary, wait. When you must act, they will open, and a way will be made through oceans and rivers, wastes and rocks.

We often make a great mistake, thinking that God is not guiding us at all, because we cannot see far in front. But this is not His method. He only undertakes that *the steps* of a good man should be ordered by the Lord. Not next year, but tomorrow. Not the next mile, but the next yard. Not the whole pattern, but the next stitch in the canvas. If you expect more than this you will be disappointed, and get back into the dark. But this will secure for you leading in the right way, as you will acknowledge when you review it from the hill-tops of glory.

We cannot ponder too deeply the lessons of the cloud given in the exquisite picture-lesson on Guidance (Numbers 9:15-23). Let us look high enough for guidance. Let us encourage our soul to wait only upon God till it is given. Let us cultivate that meekness which He will guide in judgment. Let us seek to be of quick understanding, that we may be apt to see the least sign of His will. Let us stand with girded loins and lighted lamps, that we may be prompt to obey. Blessed are those servants. They shall be led by a right way to the golden city of the saints.

Speaking for myself, after months of waiting and prayer, I have become absolutely sure of the Guidance of my heavenly Father; and with the emphasis of personal experience, I would encourage each troubled and perplexed soul that may read these lines to wait patiently for the Lord, until He clearly indicates His will.

15

Burdens, and What to do with Them

Do you keep the Sabbath? Not indeed the literal seventh-day rest, but the inner rest of which that day was the blessed type. The pause in the outward business of life was but a parable of that inner hush, which is not for one day but for all days; not for one race but for all men; not for the Hereafter only but for Now. The Sabbath-keeping which awaits the people of God, undiminished in a single atom by the storms which have swept around it, is for all faithful souls, who may take it when they will and carry it with them

'Through dusky lane and wrangling mart,
Plying their daily task with busier feet,
Because their secret souls a holy strain repeat.'

A strain borrowed from the eternal chords and harmonies of the life and being of God!

But the Secret of Sabbath-keeping is in the absence of burden-bearing. 'Thus saith the Lord, Take heed to yourselves and bear no burden on the Sabbath day, nor bring it in by the gates of Jerusalem. Neither carry forth a burden out of your houses on the Sabbath day.' And in the words that follow the continual presence of a king is made to hinge on obedience about burdens (Jeremiah 17:24 etc.). Nehemiah was so urgent in this matter, that he set his servants at the city gates, as they crowned the grey summit of Zion, 'that there should be no burden brought in on the Sabbath day' (Nehemiah 13:19).

And what was true in those bygone days is true always. There can be no true Sabbath-keeping when burdens are freely brought into the precincts of the soul. As well try to sleep when a party of high-spirited healthy children are tearing up and down the house, and playing hide-and-seek in all the rooms. Care will break the rest of the soul as much as sin does. And there is no hope that we should know the peace which passeth all understanding till we have learnt the art of shutting the door against the long train of burden-carrying thoughts which are always coming up the hill from the world beneath to fill our spirit with the ring of their feet and the clamour of their cries.

We need not stay to describe the results which burden-bearing brings to the heavy-laden. They are evident in the careworn look, the weary eye, the heavy step. But deeper than these, there is no power in prayer, no joy in God, no lying down in green pastures, no walking beside the waters of rest. As snowflakes in the arctics, or sand-grains in the tropics, will build a rampart before some lowly dwelling sufficient to exclude the light, so will worries, each of which is infinitesimal in itself, shut out the blessed light of God from the soul and make midnight where God meant midday.

And burden-bearing sadly dishonours God. As men of the world look upon the faces of those who profess to be God's children, and see them dark with the same shadows as are flung athwart their own, they may well wonder what sort of a Father He is. Whatever be a man's professions, we cannot help judging him by the faces of his children. And if God be judged by the unconscious report made of Him by some of His children, the hardest things ever said against Him by His foes are not far off the truth.

Under such circumstances the unbeliever may fitly argue, 'Either there is no God, or He is powerless to help, or He does not really love, or He is careless of the needs of His children. Of what good will religion be to me?'

We are either libels or Bibles; harbour-lights or warning-signals; magnetic or repellent; and which very much depends on how we treat our burdens.

Of course there is a difference between Care and Pain; between bearing the self-made burden of our anxieties, and suffering according to the will of God. We must not make light of sufferings sent by our Father to teach lessons which could only be learnt in the school, on the forms of which our Lord has sat before us to learn obedience. The chastened spirit must go softly, and withdraw itself to suffer. But this is very different from burden-bearing. There will be no doubt as to the Father's care, no worry about the issues, no foreboding as to the long future, which to the eye of faith gleams like the horizon-rim of the sea on which the sun is shining in splendour, though dark clouds brood immediately overhead.

Before we are thoroughly awake in the morning we sometimes become conscious of a feeling of depression, as if all were not right; and a voice seems to tell a long tale of burdens to be carried, and difficulties to be met as the hours pass by.

'Ah!' says the voice, 'a miserable day will *this* be.'

'How so?' we inquire fearfully.

'Remember, there is that creditor to meet, that skein to disentangle, that irritation to soothe, those violent tempers to confront. It is no use praying; better linger where you are, and then drag through the day as you can. You are like a martyr being led to his death.'

And too often we have yielded to the suggestion, and have dragged ourselves wearily through the hours, doing our daily task with hands engaged and strength spent by the burdens which we have assumed. God is pledged to give strength for all duties which He sets, but not for the burdens which we elect to take on as well.

The one cure for burden-bearing is to cast all burdens on the Lord. The margin of the Revised version of Psalm 55:22 reads thus: *Cast that He hath given thee upon the Lord.* Whatever burden the Lord hath given thee, give it back to Him. Treat the burden of care as once the burden of sin; kneel down and deliberately hand it over to Jesus. Say to Him, 'Lord, I entrust to Thee this, and this, and this; I cannot carry them, they are crushing me; but I definitely commit them all to Thee to manage, and adjust, and arrange. Thou hast taken my sins, take my sorrows, and in exchange give me Thy Peace, Thy Rest.' As George Herbert says so quaintly, 'We must put them all into Christ's bag.'

Will not our Lord Jesus be at least as true and faithful as the best earthly friend we have ever known? And have there not been times in all our lives when we have been too weary or helpless to help ourselves, and have thankfully handed some wearing anxiety to a good strong man, sure that when once it was entrusted to him, he would not rest until he had finished it to his satisfaction? And surely He who loved us enough to die for us may be trusted to arrange all the smaller matters of our daily lives?

Of course there are one or two conditions which we must fulfil, before we shall be able to hand over our burdens to the Lord Jesus, and leave them with Him in perfect confidence. We must have cast our sins on Him before we can cast our cares. We must be at peace with God through the work of our Saviour before we can have the peace of God through faith in His gracious interposition on our behalf. We must also be living in God's plan, tarrying under the cloud, obeying His laws and executing His plans so far as we know them. We must also feed Faith with Promise, for this food is essential to make it thrive. And when we have done all this we shall not find it so difficult

'To kneel, and cast our load,
E'en while we pray, upon our God,
Then rise with lightened cheer.'

(1) Hand over to Christ the Burden of How to Grow in Grace

This is a very great burden to some earnest people. They go from convention to convention, from one speaker to another, notebook in hand, so eager to get the Blessing (as they term it) and often thinking more of the rapture of the Gift than of the Person of the Giver. And because they hear of others having experiences which they know not, they carry heavy burdens of disappointment and self-reproach.

Equally well might a child in the infant class fret because he is not entered in the higher classes of the school. But why should he worry about his future progress? His one business is to acquire the lessons set him by his teacher. When these are learnt it will be *for him* to teach his pupil more, and advance him to positions where quicker progress may be made. And it is for us to learn the lessons which the Lord Jesus sets before us day by day, leaving Him to lead us into the fuller knowledge and love of God.

Thomas was one of the dull pupils in our Master's school. He could not see what was clear to all beside. But instead of chiding him, and leaving him to grope in the dark, the Master paid him a special visit, and made the glad fact of His resurrection so simple that the doubter was able to rejoice with the rest. Don't worry about your dullness; it will only mean that the dear Master will give you longer and more personal attention. Mothers give most pains to the sickly, weak, and stupid among their children.

(2) Hand over to Christ the Burden of maintaining a Christian Profession

Many are kept from identifying themselves openly with the Lord's people by a secret feeling that they will never be able to hold out. They carry with them a nervous dread of bringing disgrace on their Christian profession, and trailing Christ's colours in the dust. Almost unconsciously, they repeat the words of David, 'I shall now perish one day by the hand of Saul.'

But anxiety about so sacred a matter as this will hide the face of Christ, as the impalpable vapour-wreaths hide the majestic, snow-capped peaks. And it is quite needless. He who saved can uphold. As is His heart of love, so is His arm of might. He is able to keep from stumbling, and present us faultless before the presence of His glory. But we shall never know the sufficiency of that keeping whilst we cling to the boat, or even keep one hand upon its side; only when we have stepped right out on the water, relying utterly on the Master's power, shall we know how blessedly and certainly He keeps what is committed to Him against that day.

We must not carry even the burden of daily abiding in Him. Let us rather trust Him to keep us trusting and abiding in Himself. He will not fail us if we do, and will answer our faith by giving us an appetite for those exercises of prayer, Bible-study and communion, which are the secrets of unbroken fellowship.

(3) Hand over to Christ the Burden of Christian Work

How to maintain our congregations; how to hold our ground amid the competition of neighbouring workers; how to sustain the vigour and efficiency of our machinery; how to adjust the differences arising between fellow and subordinate workers; how to find material enough for sermons and addresses - beneath the pressure of burdens like these how many workers break down? They could bear the work, but not the worry.

And yet the responsibility of the work is not ours but our Master's. He is bearing this world in His arms, as a mother her sick child. He is ministering to the infinite need of man. He is carrying on His great redemptive scheme for the glory of His Father. All He wants of us is a faithful performance of the daily tasks He gives. Let the sailor-lad sleep soundly in his hammock; the captain knows exactly the ship's course. Let the errand-boy be content to fetch and carry, as he is bidden; the heads of the firm know what they are about, and have plenty of resources to meet all their needs. And let the Christian worker guard against bearing burdens which the Lord alone can carry. The Lord would never have sent us to His work without first calculating His ability to carry us through.

(4) Hand over to Christ the Burden of the Ebb and Flow of Feeling

Our feelings are as changeable as April weather. They are affected by an infinite number of subtle causes - our

144

physical health, the state of the atmosphere, over-weariness, want of sleep - as well as by those which are spiritual and inward. No stringed instrument is more liable to be affected by minute changes than we are. And we are apt to take it sorely to heart when we see the tide of emotion running fast out.

At such times we should question ourselves to see whether our lack of feeling is due to conscious sin or worrying; and if not, we may hand over all further anxiety in the matter to Him who knows our frame, and remembers that we are dust. And as we pass down the dark staircase, let us hold fast to the handrail of His will, willing still to do His will, though in the dark. 'I am as much Thine own, equally devoted to Thee now in the depths of my soul, as when I felt happiest in Thy love.'

(5) Hand over to Christ all other Burdens
Servants with their frequent changes; employers with unreasonable demands; unkind gossip and slanderous tales which are being circulated about you; the perplexities and adversities of business; the difficulty to make two ends meet; the question of changing your residence, or situation, and obtaining another; children with the ailments of childhood and the waywardness of youth; provision for sickness and old age. There are some whose businesses are peculiarly trying, and liable to cause anxious thoughts; others whose horizon is always bounded by the gaunt spectres of beggary and the workhouse.

But any one of these will break our rest, as one yelping dog may break our slumber in the stillest night, and as one grain of dust in the eye will render it incapable of enjoying the fairest prospect.

There is nothing for us, then, but to roll our burden, and indeed, ourselves, on God (Psalm 22:8 marg.). When a little boy, trying to help his father move some books, fell on the stairs beneath the weight of a heavy volume, the father ran to his aid and caught up boy and burden both, and bore them in his arms to his own room. And will our Father do worse? He must love us infinitely, and be ever at hand. 'He careth for you.'

It is a good way in dealing with God, and if you are not quite sure of His will, to say that you will stay where you are, or go on doing what you have been doing, until He makes quite clear what He wants and empowers you to do it. Roll the responsibility of your way on God (Proverbs 16:3 marg.) and expect that He will make known to you any alteration which He desires in a way so unmistakable, that though you are dull and stupid you may not mistake.

Don't worry about dress or ornaments, or doubtful things. Satan loves to turn the soul's attention from Christ to itself. It is as if a girl should spend an hour in her room wondering in what dress to meet her lover, who is waiting impatiently below. Let her go to him, and, if she desires it, he will soon enough tell her clearly what he prefers. Get into the presence of Jesus, and you will not be left to hazy questionings and doubtful disputations, but will be told clearly and unmistakably His will, and always definitely about one point at a time.

Archbishop Leighton sweetly says: 'When thou art either to do or suffer anything, when thou art about any purpose of business, go, tell God about it, and acquaint Him with it - yea, burden Him with it - and thou hast done for matter of caring. No more care, but sweet quiet diligence in thy duty, and dependence on Him for the carriage of thy matters. Roll over on God, make one bundle of all; roll thy cares, and thyself with them, as one burden, all on thy God.'

And so, when no burdens are brought into the soul, but are handed immediately over to the blessed Lord, the peace of God will fill the inner temple. And though outside there may be the strife of tongues, and the chafe of this restless world, like the troubled sea when it cannot rest, and the pressure of many engagements, yet these things shall expend themselves on the battlements of the life which is the environing presence of God; whilst, within, the soul keeps an unbroken Sabbath, like the unruffled ocean depths, which are not stirred by the hurricanes that churn the surface into foam and fury. 'The Peace of God, which passeth all understanding, shall garrison your hearts and minds through Christ Jesus' (Philippians 4:7).

16

The Stewardship of Money

The blessed truth of consecration to the Lord Jesus is spreading among Christians, as dawn over the sky which it decks with opal and amethyst. And many are discovering the true law of their being in confessing themselves *the slaves of Jesus Christ*. The blood of His Cross was not only our expiation, but our purchase-money. We are not our own, we are bought with a price. Every throb of our pulse, every faculty of our nature, every possession that we hold, is not ours, but His. So that each of us may nail up over the door of our being the words which St Paul uttered amid the dash of the storm, '*Whose I am, and whom I serve*'.

But this sort of talk must be very carefully watched. If it is true, it is the most glorious position that a human being can assume, and it will make life one long summer day of blessedness. But if it is not true, then to use such expressions will soon cauterize the conscience and sere the heart. And it becomes us, O Christian souls, to take stock of ourselves now and again, and test ourselves to see whether these words are simply pious expletives in which we lazily indulge or whether they embody the governing principle of our lives. An apostle may become an apostate, if he trifle with holy things.

One of our commonest experiences is the handling of money. And nothing will sooner show whether our consecration be a reality or a sham, nor will anything serve more quickly to accentuate and enforce the life of consecration, than to spend our money daily beneath the sway of those principles, which it is so easy to enunciate and so difficult to practise.

We have no right to look on money as our absolute property. On every coin in your possession you may read the letters D G, by the grace of God. Every coin is yours as the gift of God; as much so as if He had literally placed it on your open palm, saying, 'Take this, my child, with your Father's love'. The reasonableness of this is evident if we remember that all things owe their existence to the makership of God. 'All that is in the heaven and in the earth is Thine.' 'Thou hast created all things, for Thy pleasure they are and were created.' 'Both riches and honour come of Thee.' And David was amply justified when, as the spokesman of his people, who had just made a marvellous offering for the house of the Lord, he said, *'Of thine own have we given Thee.'*

You tell me you earn your money by the sweat of your brow. Every penny is the result of the putting forth of your muscular or mental power. Granted; but 'thou shalt remember the Lord thy God; for it is He that giveth thee power to get wealth'. He wards off paralysing disease. He maintains the mind in perfect balance. Were He to touch the sinew of your strength, instantly you would become helpless to do another stroke to bring grist to the mill.

Besides, is it not our daily profession that we have devoted ourselves, with all we are and we have, to Him? Just as many a loving wife, richly dowered, prefers to have no distinction between her own property and her husband's, and makes all over to his name, so we have professed to give ourselves and our all to Christ. We have taken His name, and our bank-books, our stocks and shares, our houses and businesses, have now written over them, in mystic characters, the initials of His name, the insignia of His glory, the brand-mark of His possession. Obviously, therefore, we have no right to look on our money as our absolute property. By our deed of gift it is His.

Is our daily practice on a level with this principle? It is a trick with little children, in a spasm of generosity, to give to those whom they love some dear possession, and to take it back again; or at least to use it without reference to the ownership they had conferred. And it is thus that too many Christians act towards Christ. They ask Him to consider all their possessions as His; but within an hour they are spending them as if they were as much their own as ever. They determine how much to give to a collection, without once asking Him what He desires. They buy any extravagant knick-knack in a shop, without considering that they have no right to spend His money in such things, without an express warrant. They make their plans for the increase of their rent, for additional and needless outlay in their homes, and for some long and expensive excursion, without laying their suggestions before their Master to know His will. Either they ought never to have professed so much, or they are cultivating a habit of unreality, which will breed disaster to themselves, and will bring shame upon their principles. If our money is really His, by His gift originally to us, and by our subsequent dedication to Him, surely He ought to have a voice in its expenditure. And the concession of that right to Him would speedily make our consecration real.

Do not suppose that it is your duty to give everything away. This would be an obvious mistake. It is our duty to provide for our own (1 Timothy 5:8) and to live in the sphere in which God has called us, and which in itself is a most precious talent (1 Corinthian 7:20). It is also clearly within our right to hold a certain amount as capital, for the increase of business and for the employment of labour. Capital may be as much considered the gift of God as any other of His gifts, and may be used for Him. And where a capitalist employs his property judiciously in furnishing work to others, taking no more of the profit than is the legitimate recompense of his time and knowledge and directing genius, and allowing his employees to share with him the common overplus; then, surely, that man is doing more real good in the world than if he gave away his property, distributing a pound each to as many poor families as he could find. But though I do not plead that consecrated Christians should give all away, I do insist upon it that they should regard all their money as Christ's, and spend every penny of it beneath His direction and in harmony with His will.

We are the Stewards of the Lord Jesus. This is His own comparison (Matthew 25:14). And it would be a happy thing if we could all come to look upon our several opportunities and faculties of doing good - power of speech, or thought, or writing, or the acquisition of money - in the same way as a faithful bailiff or steward looks on his master's goods.

May not the case be truly stated thus? Suppose that you are a man of large landed estates or other property. Circumstances compel you to go for an indefinite period beyond the seas. Before you go, you summon your steward, in whom you place implicit trust; and tell him that every quarter, when he has collected the rents and received the ordinary revenue, he may deduct from them the amount which he requires for the comfortable maintenance and education of his family, and for all needful expenditure;

and that he shall expend the whole of the remainder for you, in helping some of your poor relations, and in forwarding other projects in which you are interested. But in a short time you find, to your grief and astonishment, that, after you had left, the man whom you trusted suddenly launched out into an immense outlay on his house and equipage, on his servants and children, vying with the great ones of the land, and doling out a miserable pittance of three pence per quarter to your relations, and of a guinea per year to your cherished institutions. Would you not feel that there had been a great breach of trust, and that instant steps should be taken to supersede the unfaithful steward in his stewardship? And yet is not this precisely the way in which many of us are treating our Lord's money today? Do not we use the bulk of it for ourselves, giving to Him and His work the chance coins, which we may be able to spare, or the subscriptions which we are obliged to give, to maintain a character amongst our fellows? And there is therefore fulfilled with respect to us some ancient words, as true today as ever, Haggai 1:2; see also Malachi 3:8-10. In how many houses and places of worship are those words being sadly verified!

What a contrast to this is supplied in the cases of others, living obscurely amongst us, but millionaires in the sight of Heaven! I have been credibly informed of one, whose income is £2,000 per annum, but who lives on £200, and administers £1,800 for the Lord's service; of another, whose income is £8,000, but who lives on £250, and gives away the remainder; of yet another, a governess, who, out of the £100 that she earns, keeps £50 and gives away the other £50; whilst another who earns £1,500, lives on £100 and exercises a wise stewardship over the rest. A friend of my own, who has long since made a comfortable competence, is remaining in business for the purpose of devoting all his profits to the cause of Christ. As surely as some have speaking or writing faculties, which they are bound to use for God's service, so others have business faculties, which they are equally required to exercise for the same purpose; not wrapping them to waste in the buried napkin. What would you think of a minister who ceased preaching for no other reason than that he had enough to live upon! And surely, if a man has no other talent than a business faculty, he had better go on employing that, rather than do nothing, for the Redeemer's glory.

There remain two or three simple rules, which may gather up into a practical shape the conclusions to which we have come.

(1) Let us consecrate ourselves afresh to our Redeemer
Let each reader of these words thoughtfully take that step which inspired David Livingstone in his mighty career! His last birthday but one was spent far away from home and friends, in the wild jungle, surrounded by those degraded Africans that lay so near his heart; and in his diary he penned these touching words: 'My Jesus, my King, my Life, my All, I again dedicate my whole self to Thee.' What better could you do than take your diary in hand, and write these very words? And if you like, add an inventory of all that you include within their embrace; and then append your signature. Remember that scene in the churchyard of the Greyfriars in Edinburgh, when the Covenanters signed their names in blood drawn from their hearts. Be as earnest as they were, and trust Christ to keep you true.

(2) Determine beneath the eye of Christ how much you should legitimately spend on yourself

There are several things to be considered, among the first of which is Life insurance. Then rent, taxes, maintenance, education and such-like. None of us can determine these things for another. They must be settled calmly under the Master's eye. Not in days of panic or pressure, for at such times we are not likely to form a correct estimate. But in times when we can quietly calculate what Christ would have us expend; always remembering that we have no right to presume on windfalls or miracles: or to provide for ostentation and excess; or to go beyond our income; or to risk running into debt. But when once we have prayerfully ascertained our position, we should maintain it, unless we have very clear tokens that we are to exchange it for another, whether better or worse. Many Christians, directly their income begins to increase, launch out into increased expenditure; whereas it may be that the increase is to be devoted to the cause of Christ. Ah! what moral ruin has come to families, because of the lavish waste of Christian homes! Other Christians, in times of straitness, begin to reduce *necessary* expenditure and to sell articles of use. It may be right to do so. But on the whole, one would need to be clearly led by God's Spirit in all such matters. It may be His will to maintain them as they are, but by other means, until prosperity is restored to them. Our only care should be to please God, and never run into debt. Leave the provision of each meal to Him who feeds the birds and clothes the flowers (Romans 13:8; Matthew 6:25).

(3) Give away a stated proportion of all you own or earn
It may seem needless to insert this caution to those who

154

should use all for Christ. But it is really most important. And for this reason. Our hearts are weak and fickle; and we are in danger of making so good a provision for ourselves, that the Lord's surplus will be next to nothing. We remember so vividly the amount we give away that it bulks up largely beyond our mind; and we imagine that we are generous, until we see in figures how small a proportion our charity bears to our income. To guard against this, it is well always to put aside a certain part for the Lord before we begin to divide up the rest, so that His share may be as safe as our rent. This will not prevent us from still considering that the whole is His, or from administering the overplus, for the furtherance of those objects that lie near His heart.

It is not within my province to say what proportion of our income we should statedly set apart for God. The patriarch gave a tenth; and surely the noon of Christianity should not inspire less benevolence than the twilight (Genesis 28:22). And it has been calculated that the Jews gave in all at least one-fifth of their income to the maintenance of their religion. But of course the proportion we can statedly set apart for Christ must vary with our circumstances. A man, when his family is young, may be able to give only a tenth, who, when his expenses are less, can as easily dedicate a fifth or a third. Let each be fully persuaded in his own mind. Only let this principle be observed, that there be a stated proportion given out of every pound, whether the income be received weekly, or monthly, or quarterly, or whether it be only realised at the end of the year. Every business man knows pretty well what his income is, else how can he fix the sum given in for income tax? Let him deal as faithfully with God as with the Government officer; or let him expend during the current

155

year a proportion of his income made during the previous one. So shall we obey the spirit at least of the Apostolic exhortation: 'Upon the first day of the week let every one of you lay by him in store as God hath prospered him' (1 Corinthians 16:2). When, then, we are called upon to give, it will be a luxury to administer wisely the Lord's money; and all the remainder will seem sanctified through the dedication of the firstfruits (Proverbs 3:9, 10).

(4) Sometimes let us make a special offering to the Lord Jesus

We can only give Him what is His. And yet, though a wife has nothing of her own, she can make presents to her husband of what he gave her, and which she might have legitimately used for herself, but which she has saved until it grew into a worthy gift for her spouse. Love must give of that which costs her something. There are no gifts so precious in the eyes of the loved one as those which mean planning and self-sacrifice. And think you not that it delights the heart of our Lord to receive at our hands love-tokens; precious ornaments and jewels; alabaster boxes, reserved once for self-adornment, but now gladly surrendered; articles of beauty and value, which we had hidden from the light of day, but which we present to Him, to show that our love is strong, personal and self-forgetting? 'He is worthy to receive riches.' And the chief zest of such gifts is in their secrecy from all human eyes; a personal transaction between the Master and the loving heart. 'That thine alms may be in secret.'

(5) Be careful to put the Lord's money aside

We must not trust in our memories, or generalities. We

must be minute, and specific, and careful, some having a bag, others a box, into which the Lord's portion is carefully put; some having a separate banking account; and all having some kind of ledger account, where we may put down what we receive and spend for Christ, that there may be no embezzlement, however inadvertent, of that which is not ours.

Of the rewards that will accrue we have no time to speak. Wasteful and harmful expenditure will be checked. Evil ways of getting money will be abandoned. Treasures will be laid up in the heavens. Bags which wax not old will be provided. The Lord's treasuries will be filled to overflowing. There will no longer be the sad refusal of young and eager hearts, because there are no funds to send them forth to their coveted life-work in distant lands. The gulf between rich and poor will be bridged by many deeds of ministry and helpfulness. Whilst, better than all, the Master's voice will ring like music through the heart, 'Well done, thou good and faithful servant; enter thou into the joy of thy Lord.'

That such a welcome, dear readers, may be addressed to each of you, is one reason why these words have been written; and another is a conviction, that many of the methods now employed to raise money for our Master's work must be exceedingly distasteful to Him; and that there are funds enough in the possession of Christians for all the needs of the Church, in her work of evangelisation, if only they were properly administered. Let us not take the tarnished gifts of the King of Sodom, but let each member of the one Church administer aright the sacred trust of money.

17

Our Bible Reading

The whole of Christian Living, in my opinion, hinges on the way in which Christian people read the Bible for themselves. All sermons and addresses, all Bible-readings and classes, all religious magazines and books, can never take the place of our own quiet study of God's precious Word. We may measure our growth in grace by the growth of our love for private Bible study. And we may be sure that there is something seriously wrong, when we lose our appetite for the Bread of Life. Perhaps we have been eating too many sweets; or taking too little exercise; or breathing too briefly in the bracing air, which sweeps over the uplands of Spiritual Communion with God.

Happy are they who have learnt the blessed art of discovering for themselves the treasures of the Bible, which are hidden just a little below the surface, so as to test our real earnestness in finding them. No specimens are so interesting as those which the Naturalist has obtained by his own exertions, and each of which has a history. No flowers are so fragrant, as those which we discover for ourselves, nestling in some woodland dell, remote from the eye and step of men. No pearls are so priceless as those which we have sought for ourselves in the calm clear depths of the ocean of truth. Only those who know it can realise the joy that fills the spirit when one has made a great 'find', in some hidden connection, some fresh reference, or some railways lines from verse to verse.

There are a few simple rules, which may help many

more to acquire this holy art, and I venture to note them down. May the Holy Spirit Himself own and use them!

(1) Make time for Bible Study

The Divine Teacher must have fixed and uninterrupted hours for meeting His scholars. His Word must have our freshest and brightest thoughts. We must give Him our best, and the first-fruits of our days. Hence there is no time for Bible study like the early morning. For we cannot give such undivided attention to the holy thoughts that glisten like diamonds on its pages after we have opened our letters, glanced through the paper, and joined in the prattle of the breakfast table. The manna had to be gathered, before the dew was off, and the sun was up; otherwise it melted.

We ought, therefore, to aim at securing, at least half an hour before breakfast, for the leisurely and loving study of the Bible. To some this may seem a long time in comparison with what they now give. But it will soon seem all too short. The more you read the Bible the more you will want to read it. It is an appetite which grows as it is fed. And you will be well repaid. The Bible seldom speaks, and certainly never its deepest, sweetest words, to those who always read it in a hurry.

Nature can only tell her secrets to such as will sit still in her sacred Temple, till their eyes lose the glare of earthly glory; and their ears are attuned to her voice. And shall Revelation do what Nature cannot? Never. The man who shall win the blessedness of hearing her must watch daily at her gates, and wait at the posts of her doors. There is no chance for a lad to grow, who only gets an occasional mouthful of food, and always swallows that in a hurry!

Of course this season before breakfast is not possible

159

for all. The Invalid, the Nurse with broken rest, the Public Servant whose night is often turned into day - these stand alone; and the Lord Jesus can make it up to them; sitting with them at midday, if needs be, beside the well. In the case of such as can only snatch a few words of Scripture as they hasten to their work, there will be repeated the miracle of the manna. 'He that gathered much had nothing over'; i.e. all we get in our morning reading is not too much for the needs of the day; 'and he that gathered too little had no lack'; i.e. when, by force of circumstances, we are unable to do more than snatch up a hasty handful of manna, it will last us all through the day; the cruse of oil shall not waste, and the barrel of meal shall not fail.

It would be impossible to name all who have traced their usefulness and power to this priceless habit. Sir Henry Havelock always spent the first two hours of each day alone with God; and if the encampment was struck at 6 am, he would rise at 4. Earl Cairns rose daily at 6 o'clock to secure an hour and a half for the study of the Bible and for prayer, before conducting family worship at a quarter to eight; even when the late hours of the House of Commons left him not more than two hours for his night's rest. It is the practice of a beloved friend, who stands in the front rank of modern Missionaries, to spend at least three hours each morning with his Bible; and he has said, that he often puts aside pressing engagements, that he may not only have time, but be fresh for it.

There is no doubt a difficulty in awakening and arising early enough to get time for our Bibles before breakfast. But these difficulties present no barrier to those who must get away early for daily business, or for the appointments of pleasure. If we mean to get up, we can get up. Of course we must prepare the way for early rising by retiring early to obtain our needed rest, though it be at the cost of some cosy hours by the fireside in the winter's night. But with due forethought and fixed purpose the thing can surely be done. 'All things are possible to him that believeth.'

I never shall forget seeing Charles Studd, early one November morning, clothed in flannels to protect him from the cold, and rejoicing that the Lord had awaked him at 4 am to study His commands. He told me then, that it was his custom to trust the Lord to call him and enable him to rise. Might not we all do this? The weakest can do all things through Christ that strengtheneth us. And though you have failed again and again when you have trusted your own resolutions, you cannot fail when you are simply trusting Him. 'He wakeneth me morning by morning.' 'He took him by the right hand, and lifted him up; and immediately his feet and ankle bones received strength.'

(2) Look up for the Teaching of the Holy Spirit

No one can so well explain the meaning of his words as he who wrote them. Tennyson could best explain some of his deeper references in 'In Memoriam'. If then, you want to read the Bible as you should, make much of the Holy Ghost who inspired it through holy men. As you open the book, lift up your heart, and say: 'Open Thou mine eyes that I may behold wondrous things out of Thy law. Speak, Lord, for Thy servant heareth.'

It is marvellous what slender light commentaries cast on the inner meaning of Scripture. A simple-hearted believer, depending on the aid of the Holy Ghost, will find things in the Bible which the wisest have mistaken or missed. Well might St John say of such, 'Ye need not that any man should teach you; but the anointing, which ye have received, teacheth you of all things.' The teaching of the Holy Ghost brings out passages in the Bible, which had seemed meaningless and bare.

We can never know too much of that literature which throws side-lights on the Bible; and which unfolds the customs of the people; difficult allusions, historical coincidences, geographical details. Geikie's *Hours with the Bible*; Kitto's *Daily Illustrations*, edited by Dr Porter; Dr Smith's *Bible Dictionary*: books like these are invaluable. But we should study them at other times than in the morning hour, reserved for the Holy Ghost alone.

(3) Read the Bible methodically
For some reason it is very helpful to map out the Bible into three Annual Courses, and then neatly insert the dates, once for all, in the margin as a permanent guide. The Old Testament forms two Annual Courses, each portion averaging five-sixths of a page of a Bagster's Bible; while the New Testament makes a single course, each day's reading being on an average exactly one column.

This system has been adopted by those members of the YMCA Bible Reading Union not already pledged to use other portions; and by other friends who use the tasteful little 'Calendars' (one for each Testament) in which the Annual Courses are clearly arranged. The short New Testament portions should be read every year by all; and *one* Old Testament course by all who can possibly do so, thus working the larger division of the Sacred Volume through in two years.

It is wise to have a good copy of the Scriptures, strongly bound for wear and tear; of good clear print, and with as much space as possible for notes. It is wise at first to select one with copious marginal references, so that it may be easy to turn to the parallel passages. For myself, this plan has invested my Bible reading with new interest. I love to have in front of me one of the Paragraph Bibles of the Religious Tract Society, which abound in well-chosen references, and a small pocket Bible in my hand, that I may easily turn to any references I desire; and very often I get more blessing from the passages to which I refer, and those to which these lead, than from the one I may be reading.

After a while, we shall begin to make references for ourselves, and then we may use a copy of the Revised Bible; that we may not only be able to read God's Word in the most approved English rendering, which is an immense advantage; but that we may also be able to fill up the empty margins with the notes of parallel passages.

But whatever system is adopted, be sure to read the Bible through on some system as you would read any other book. No one would think of reading a letter, poem, or history, as many read God's Word. What wonder that they are so ignorant of its majestic prose, its exquisite lyric poetry, its massive arguments, its sublime imagery, its spiritual beauty - qualities which combine to make it the King of Books, even though the halo of Inspiration did not shine like a crown about its brow!

It is sometimes well to read a book at a sitting, devoting two or three hours to the sacred task. At other times, it is more profitable to take an epoch, or an episode, or a life, and compare all that is written of it in various parts of Scripture. At other times, again, it is well to follow the plan, on which Mr Moody has so often insisted, of taking one word or thought, as Faith, or Love, or Able, and tracing it, by help of a concordance, from end to end of the inspired volume. But in any case, let the *whole* Bible be your study; because '*All* Scripture is given by inspiration of God, and is profitable'. Even the rocky places shall gush with water-springs. The most barren chapters shall blossom as the rose. 'Out of the eater shall come forth meat, and sweetness out of the strong.'

Let us never forget that the Bible is one Book, the work of one Infinite Spirit, speaking through Prophet and Priest, Shepherd and King, the old-world Patriarch and the Apostle who lived to see Jerusalem levelled to the ground. You may subject its words to the most searching test, but you will find they will always bear the same meaning, and move in the same direction. Let the Bible be its own Dictionary, its own Interpreter, its own best Commentary. It is like a vast buried city, in which every turn of the spade reveals some new marvel, whilst passages branch off in every direction calling for exploration.

(4) Read your Bible with your pen in hand

Writing of F R Havergal, her sister says, 'She read her Bible at her study table by seven o'clock in the summer, and eight o'clock in winter; sometimes on bitterly cold mornings. I begged that she would read with her feet comfortably to the fire, and received the reply: "But then, Marie, I can't rule my lines neatly; just see what a find I've got!" If only one searches, there are such extraordinary things in the Bible. She resolutely refrained from late hours and frittering tasks at night in place of Bible searchings and holy communings. Early rising and early studying were her rule through life.'

None, in my judgement, have learned the secret of

enjoying the Bible until they have commenced to mark it, neatly. Underlining and dating special verses, which have cast a light upon their path on special days. Drawing railway connections across the page between verses, which repeat the same message or ring with the same note. Jotting down new references, or the catch-words of helpful thoughts. All these methods find plenty of employment for the pen and fix our treasures for us permanently. Our Bible then becomes the precious memento of bygone hours; and records the history of our inner life.

(5) Seek eagerly your personal profit

Do not read the Bible for others, for class or congregation; but for yourself. Bring all its rays to a focus on your own heart. Whilst you are reading often ask that some verse or verses may start out from the printed page, as God's message to yourself. And never close the book until you feel that you are carrying away your portion of meat from that Hand which satisfieth the desire of every living thing. It is well sometimes to stop reading, and seriously ask, What does the Holy Spirit mean *me* to learn by this; what bearing should this have on *my* life; how can I work this into the fabric of *my* character?

Let not the Bible be to you simply as a history, a treatise, or a poem, but as your Father's letter to yourself, in which there are some things which you will not understand, till you come into the circumstances which require them; but which is also full of present help. There is a great difference between the way in which an absent child scans the parcel of newspapers, and that in which he devours the Home-letter, by which the beloved parent speaks. Both are interesting, but the one is general, the other is all to himself.

Read the Bible, not as a newspaper, but as a Home-letter.

Above all, turn from the printed page to prayer. If a cluster of heavenly fruit hangs within reach, gather it. If a promise lies upon the page as a blank cheque, cash it. If a prayer is recorded, appropriate it, and launch it as a feathered arrow from the bow of your desire. If an example of holiness gleams before you, ask God to do as much for you. If a truth is revealed in all its intrinsic splendour, entreat that its brilliance may ever irradiate the hemisphere of your life like a star. Entwine the climbing creepers of holy desire about the lattice work of Scripture. So shall you come to say with the Psalmist, 'Oh, how I love Thy law, it is my meditation all the day!'

It is sometimes well to read over, on our knees, Psalm 119, so full of devout love for the Bible. And if any should chide us for spending so much time upon the Old Testament, or the New, let us remind them of the words of Christ, 'Man shall not live by bread alone, but by every word that proceedeth out of the mouth of God.' The Old Testament must be worth our study since it was our Saviour's Bible, deeply pondered and often quoted. And the New demands it, since it is so full of what He said, and did, not only in His earthly life, but through the medium of His holy apostles and prophets.

The advantages of a deep knowledge of the Bible are more than can be numbered here. It is the Storehouse of the Promises. It is the Sword of the Spirit before which temptation flees. It is the all-sufficient Equipment for Christian usefulness. It is the believer's Guidebook and Directory in all possible circumstances. Words fail to tell how glad, how strong, how useful shall be the daily life of those who can say with the Prophet, 'Thy words were found, and I did eat them; and Thy word was unto me the joy and rejoicing of my heart.'

But there is one thing, which may be said last, because it is most important, and should linger in the memory and heart, though all the other exhortations of this chapter should pass away as a summer brook. It is this. It is useless to dream of making headway in the knowledge of Scripture, unless we are prepared to practise each new and clearly-defined duty, which looms out before our view. We are taught, not for our pleasure only, *but that we may do*. If we will turn each holy precept or command into instant obedience, through the dear grace of Jesus Christ our Lord, God will keep nothing back from us; He will open to us His deepest and sweetest thoughts. But so long as we refuse obedience to even the least command, we shall find that the light will fade from the page of Scripture, and the zest will die down quickly in our own hearts.

'This Book of the Law shall not depart out of thy mouth, but thou shalt meditate therein day and night, that thou mayest observe to do according to all that is written therein: for then thou shalt make thy way prosperous, and then thou shalt have good success' (Joshua 1:8).

18

'In a Strait, Betwixt Two'
(Philippians 1:23)

> *'With the patriarch's joy*
> *Thy call I follow to the Land unknown;*
> *I trust in Thee, and know in whom I trust;*
> *Or life or death is equal - neither weighs!*
> *All weight in this - oh, let me live to Thee!'*
>
> *(Young)*

Through the providence of God, and probably by the kind
intervention of the centurion - who had conceived a sincere
admiration for him during these months of travel together,
and who, indeed, owed him his life - Paul, on his arrival in
Rome, was treated with great leniency. He was permitted
to hire a house or apartment in the near neighbourhood of
the great Pretorian barracks, and live by himself, the only
sign of his captivity consisting in the chain that fastened his
wrist to a Roman legionary, the soldiers relieving each
other every four or six hours.

There were many advantages in this arrangement. It
secured him from the hatred of his people, and gave him a
marvellous opportunity of casting the seeds of the gospel
into the head of the rivers of population, that poured from
the metropolis throughout the known world. At the same
time, it must have been very irksome. Always to be in the
presence of another, and that other filled with Gentile
antipathy to Jewish habits and pagan irresponsiveness to
Christian fervour; to be able to make no movement without

the clanking of his chain, and the consent of his custodian; to have to conduct his conferences, utter his prayers, and indite his epistles, beneath those stolid eyes, or amid brutal and blasphemous interruptions - all this must have been excessively trying to a sensitive temperament like the Apostle's. That must have been a hard and long schooling, which had taught him to be content even with this, for the sake of the gospel. But this, also, he could do through Christ that strengthened him. And it also turned out greatly to the furtherance of the cause he loved. Many of these brawny veterans became humble, earnest disciples. With a glow of holy joy, he informs the Philippians that his bonds in Christ have become manifest throughout the whole Pretorian guard (1:13); and we know that this was the beginning of a movement destined within three centuries to spread throughout the entire army, and compel Constantine to adopt Christianity as the religion of the State. This was a blessed issue of that period of suffering which so often extorted the cry, 'Remember my bonds.'

Three days after his arrival in Rome, Paul summoned to his temporary lodging the leaders of the Jewish synagogues, of which there are said to have been seven, for the 60,000 Jews who were the objects of the dislike and ridicule of the imperial city. At the first interview they cautiously occupied neutral ground, and expressed the wish to hear and judge for themselves, concerning the sect which was only known to them as the butt of universal execration. At the second interview, after listening to Paul's explanations and appeals for an entire day, there was the usual division of opinion. 'Some believed the things that were spoken, and some believed not.' His testimony having thus been first offered, according to his invariable practice, to his own people, there was now no further obstacle to his addressing a wider audience. The message of salvation was sent to the Gentiles, and these would certainly hear. We are not, therefore, surprised to be told that for the next two years, whilst his accusers were preparing their case, or the emperor was permitting shameless indulgence to interfere with the discharge of public business, 'He received all that went in unto him, preaching the Kingdom of God, and teaching the things concerning the Lord Jesus Christ with all boldness, none forbidding him' (Acts 28:17-30).

It might be said of the Apostle, as of his Lord, that they came to him from every quarter. Timothy, his son in the faith; Mark, now 'profitable'; Luke, with his quick physician's eye and delicate sympathy; Aristarchus, who shared his imprisonment, that he might have an opportunity of ministering to his needs; Tychicus from Ephesus, 'the beloved brother and faithful minister in the Lord'; Epaphras from Colossae, a 'beloved fellow-servant, and faithful minister of Christ', on the behalf of the church there; Epaphroditus from Philippi, who brought the liberal contributions of the beloved circle, that for so many years had never ceased to remember their friend and teacher; Demas, who had not yet allowed the present to turn him aside from the eternal and unseen - these, and others, are mentioned in the postscripts of his Epistles as being with him. Members of the Roman church would always be welcomed, and must have poured into his humble lodging in a perpetual stream; Epaenetus and Mary, Andronicus and Junia, Tryphena and Tryphosa, Persis the beloved, and Apelles the approved, must often have resorted to that apartment, which was irradiated with the perpetual presence of the Lord. They had come to meet him on his first arrival as far

170

as the Appii Forum and the Three Taverns, and would not be likely to neglect him, now he was settled among them.

Then what interest would be aroused by the episodes of those two years! The illness of Epaphroditus, who was sick unto death; the discovery and conversion of Onesimus, the runaway slave; the writing and despatch of the Epistles, which bear such evident traces of the prison cell. There could have been no lack of incident, amid the interest of which the two years must have sped by more swiftly than the other two years spent in confinement at Caesarea.

It is almost certain that Paul was acquitted at his first trial, and liberated, and permitted for two or three years at least to engage again in his beloved work. He was evidently expecting this, when, writing to the Philippians, he said: 'I myself am confident in the Lord, that I myself, too, shall come speedily' (2:24). In his letter to Philemon also, he goes so far as to ask that a lodging may be prepared for him, as he hopes to be granted to their prayers. Universal tradition affirms an interspace of liberty between his two imprisonments; and without this hypothesis, it is almost impossible to explain many of the incidental allusions of the Epistles to Timothy and Titus, which cannot refer, so far as we can see, to the period that falls within the compass of the Acts.

Whether his liberation were due to the renewed offices of the centurion, or to more explicit reports received from Caesarea, history does not record; but it was by the decree of a greater than Nero that the coupling-chain was struck off the Apostle's wrist, and he was free to go where he would. That he should abide in the flesh was, in the eye of the great Head of the Church, needful for the furtherance and joy of faith to the little communities that looked to him as their father; and their rejoicing was destined to be more abundant in Jesus Christ by his coming to them again.

Once more a free man, Paul would certainly fulfil his intention of visiting Philemon and the church of Colossae. Thence he would make his way to the church at Ephesus, to hold further converse with them on those sacred mysteries which in his Epistle he had commenced to unfold. It was probably during his residence there that Onesiphorus ministered to him with such tender thoughtfulness as to elicit a significant reference in the last Epistle (2 Timothy 1:18). Leaving Timothy behind him with the injunction to command some that they should preach no other gospel than they had heard from his lips (1 Timothy 1:3), he travelled onward to Macedonia and Philippi. What a greeting must have been accorded to him there! They were his brethren, beloved and longed for, his joy and crown, whom he ever held in his heart, and who in the defence and confirmation of the gospel had so deeply partaken with him. Lydia and Clement, Euodia and Syntyche, Epaphroditus and the gaoler, together with many other fellow-workers whose names are in the Book of Life, must have gathered around to minister to that frail, worn body, to be inspired by that heroic soul.

From Philippi he must have passed to other churches in Greece, and amongst the rest to Corinth. Finally he set sail with Titus for Crete, where he left him to set in order the things that were wanting, and to appoint elders in every city (Titus 1:5). On his return to the mainland he wrote an epistle to Titus, from the closing messages in which we gather that he was about to winter at Nicopolis surrounded by several friends, such as Artemas, Zenas, Tychicus and Apollos, who were inspired with his own spirit, and were

172

gladly assisting him in strengthening the organisation and purifying the teaching in these young churches, each of which had possibly to pass through some such phases of doctrinal and practical difficulty as are reflected in the mirror of the Epistles to Corinth (1 Corinthians 3:12, 13).

This blessed liberty, however, was summarily cut short. One of the most terrible events in the history of the ancient world - the burning of Rome - took place in the year AD 64; and to divert from himself the suspicion which indicated him as its author, Nero accused the Christians of being the incendiaries. Immediately the fierce flames of the first general persecution broke out. Those who were resident in the metropolis, and who must have been well known and dear to the Apostle, were seized and subjected to horrible barbarities, whilst a strict search was made throughout the empire for their leaders, the Jews abetting the inquisitors. It was not likely that so eminent a Christian as the Apostle would escape. The storm that sweeps the forest will smite first and most destructively the loftiest trees.

He was staying for a time at Troas, in the house of Carpus, where he had arrived from Nicopolis. His arrest was so sudden that he had not time to gather up his precious books and parchments, which may have included copies of his Epistles, a Hebrew Bible, and some early copies of the sayings of our Lord; or to wrap around him the cloak which had been his companion in many a wintry storm. Thence he was hurried to Rome.

A little group of friends accompanied him, with faithful tenacity, in this last sad journey. Demas and Crescens, Titus and Tychicus, Luke and Erastus. But Erastus abode at Corinth, through which the little band may have passed; and Trophimus fell ill at Miletus, and had to be left there, as the Roman guard would brook no delay (2 Timothy 4:20). So, for the second time, Paul reached Rome.

But the circumstances of his second imprisonment differed widely from those of the first. Then he had his own hired house; now he was left in close confinement, and tradition points to the Mamertine prison as the scene of his last weeks or months. Then he was easily accessible; now Onesiphorus had to seek him out very diligently, and it took some courage not to be ashamed of his chain. Then he was the centre of a large circle of friends and sympathisers; now the winnowing fan of trouble had greatly thinned their ranks, whilst others had been despatched on distant missions. 'Only Luke is with me' is the rather sad expression of the old man's loneliness (2 Timothy 4:11). Then he cherished a bright hope of speedy liberation; now, though he had successfully met the first impeachment, which was probably one of incendiarism, and had been delivered out of the mouth of the lion, he had no hope of meeting the second, which would include the general charge of introducing new customs hostile to the stability of the imperial government. Its very vagueness made it so hard to combat, and it was inevitable that he should be caught within its meshes.

He was already being poured out as a libation, and the time had come for his loosing the anchor and setting sail. But it caused him no sorrow. In earlier days he had greatly set his heart on being clothed upon with the body that was from heaven, and on being suddenly caught up to be for ever with the Lord. It seemed unlikely now that such would be the method of his transition to that rest of which he had spoken so pathetically. Not by the triumphant path of the air, but by the darksome path of death and the grave, would

174

he pass into the presence of the Lord. It was, however, a matter of small importance what would be the method of his home-going; he was only too thankful, on his review of his career, to say humbly and truthfully, 'I have striven the good strife, I have finished my course, I have kept the faith; henceforth there is laid up for me a crown of righteousness' (2 Timothy 4:7).

How characteristic it is to find him boasting of the great audience of Gentiles, to whom, at the first stage of his trial, he was able fully to proclaim the gospel message. It is equally characteristic to hear him affirm that the ease and success of his witness-bearing was due, not to himself, but to the conscious nearness of his Lord, who stood by and strengthened him (2 Timothy 4:16-17).

What were the following processes of the trial? How long was he kept in suspense? Did Timothy arrive in time to see him, and to be with him at the last supreme moment? What was the exact method of his martyrdom? To these questions there is no certain reply. Tradition points to a spot, about three miles from Rome on the Ostian road, where, at the stroke of the headsman's axe, he was beheaded, and his spirit leaving its frail tenement, entered the house not made with hands, eternal in the heavens.

But how vast the contrast between that scene which may have excited but little interest save to the friends that mingled in the little group, and that other scene in which an abundant entrance was ministered to this noble spirit as it entered the presence of the Lord! If Christ arose to receive Stephen, may He not also have stood up to welcome Paul? Again he beheld the face that had looked down on him from the opened heavens at his conversion and heard the voice that had called him by his name. His long-cherished wish of being 'with Christ' was gratified, and he found it 'far better' than he had ever thought.

His was now the inheritance of the saints in light, of which the Holy Spirit had been the earnest and firstfruits. He had passed the goal and had attained to the prize of his high calling in Christ. He had been found in Christ not having his own righteousness, but the righteousness which is of God by faith. No castaway was he! As he had kept Christ's deposit, so Christ had kept his. And as he gave in the account of his stewardship, who can doubt that the Lord greeted him with, 'Well done, good and faithful servant, enter thou into the joy of thy Lord.'

What a festal welcome he must have received from thousands whom he had turned from darkness to light, from the power of Satan unto God, and who were now to become his crown of rejoicing in the presence of the Lord! These from the highlands of Galatia, and those from the seaboard of Asia Minor. These from Judaistic prejudice, and those from the depths of Gentile depravity and sin. These from the degraded slave populations, and those from the ranks of the high-born and educated. Nor have such greetings ceased; but through all the centuries that have succeeded there are comparatively few that have passed along 'the Way to the Celestial City' who have not had to acknowledge a deep debt of gratitude to him who, of all others, was enabled to give a clearer apprehension of the Divine method of justifying and saving sinners.

What share the blessed ones within the veil may have in hastening the Second Advent we cannot tell. But, surely, among those who eagerly anticipate that hour when the Bridegroom shall present the church to Himself, without spot or wrinkle or any such thing, there is none more eager than he, who looked so constantly, even to the end, for the blessed hope, the appearance of the glorious Saviour, and who did so much to prepare the church for her Lord! And, among the stones of the foundations of the New Jerusalem, on which are written the names of the twelve Apostles of the Lamb, will surely be found at last that of Saul, also called Paul, who was before a blasphemer, a persecutor, and injurious, but who obtained mercy and was counted faithful.

19

'How Large Letters'
(Galatians 6:11)

*'All his glowing language issued forth
With God's deep stamp upon its current worth'*
(Cowper)

It has been supposed, with much show of reason, that at the
close of the Epistle to the Galatians, the Apostle took the
pen from the hand of his amanuensis and wrote somewhat
more than his usual brief autograph. Generally he con-
tented himself with such words as those with which the
Epistle to the Colossians closes, 'The salutation of me,
Paul, with mine own hand. Remember my bonds. Grace be
with you.' But in the case of the Galatians, among whom
his authority had been greatly impugned, it seemed incumbent to give rather more emphasis and importance to his
words by a prolonged personal closing paragraph. He
practically begs them excuse the clumsy shape and appearance of his handwriting, on account of his defective sight;
to which he may also be alluding when he touchingly
describes himself as branded with the marks of Jesus
(Galatians 6:17).

We must take his words also in a metaphoric sense.
How largely his letters bulk in the make-up of the New
Testament! If we judge the question only by comparing
their length with that of the New Testament, we shall find
that they make a fourth part of the whole. And their importance must be measured not by length but by weight.

Before you put them into the scale, consider the precious treasures you are handling. The sublime chapter on Love, 1 Corinthians 13; the matchless argument on Justification in Romans 4, 5; the glorious exposition of the work of the Holy Spirit in Romans 8; the triumphant Resurrection Hope of 1 Corinthians 15; the tender unveiling of the Love between Jesus and his own in Ephesians 5 - what priceless treasures are these which the Church owes first to the Holy Ghost, and next to the Apostle Paul, acting as His organ and instrument. How many of the most precious and helpful passages in Scripture bear the mark of the tender, eager, fervent and devout spirit of the Apostle of the Gentiles.

The Epistles marvellously reflect his personality. It has been said of one of the great painters that he was wont to mix his colours with blood drawn from a secret wound; and of Paul it may be said that he dipped his pen in the blood of his heart. Whatever impression had last rested on his sensitive nature coloured the flow of his thoughts and expressions, whether it was Philippian love expressed by the coming of Epaphroditus, or the story of the Corinthian division told by the members of the house of Chloe. Probably it is for this very reason, because he wrote with all the freshness of speech, with the sparkle of conversation, as though he was talking naturally in a circle of friends, that he has so moved the heart of the world.

But it is not too much to say that, humanly speaking, the gospel of Christ would never have taken such fast hold on the strong, practical, vigorous nations of the West, had it not been for these Epistles. The mind of the Apostle John is given to deep and spiritual insight, which sees, rather than argues, its way into the truths of the gospel. The mind of the Apostle Peter, again, is specially Hebraic: he looks at everything from the standpoint of his early education and training, on which the teachings of his Master had been grafted. But with Paul, though he writes as a Hebrew of the Hebrews, employing methods of Scripture interpretation, which, being in the method of the Rabbis, are recondite and unfamiliar to our thought, yet his Epistles are characterised by a virility, a logical order, a style of argument, a definiteness of statement and phraseology, which are closely akin to our Western civilisation. When he was born the Roman Empire was in the summer of its glory, and Greek culture so infused into the universal thought and speech, that even the exclusivism and bigotry of the Jewish ghettos were not wholly proof against it. The breath of the Western ocean is in these Epistles; the tides of the coming centuries were already rolling into the estuary, and causing the barges of long stationary tradition to move uneasily and rattle their mooring-chains. It is for this reason that Paul has been the contemporary of Western civilisation through all the centuries. It was he who taught Augustine and inspired Luther. His thoughts and conceptions have been wrought into the texture, and woven into the woof of the foremost minds of the Christian centuries. The seeds he scattered have fruited in the harvests of modern education, jurisprudence, liberty and civilisation.

'Ah!' it has been eloquently said, 'what does the world owe to this Apostle; what has it owed to him; what will it owe; of pious pastors, zealous missionaries, eminent Christians, useful books, benevolent endowments, examples of faith, charity, purity, holiness? Who can calculate it? The whole human race will arise and confess that amongst all the names of its benefactors whom it is pleased to enrol from age to age, there is no one whom it proclaims with so much harmony, gratitude and love, as the name of the Apostle Paul.'

We have thirteen Letters bearing the inscription and signature of Paul. The evidence of their genuineness and authenticity is generally admitted; even the extreme school of destructive criticism has been compelled to admit that the Epistles to the Corinthians, Galatians and Romans are undoubtedly his. They were written at different periods between the years 52 and 68 AD; and under very different circumstances. These when hope was young and fresh in the first glad dawn; these amid the stress of strong antagonism; these with the shackles of the prison on the wrist; these when the sun was dyeing the horizon with its last intense glow. Each largely tinctured with the complexion of the worlds without and within, but all full of that devotion to the risen Lord which led him to subscribe himself so often as his devoted bond-servant. 'Paul, the bond-servant of Jesus Christ.'

Let us place these Epistles in the order of their composition, and see how they mark the successive stages of progress in the Apostle's conceptions of Christ. He was always full of Love and Loyalty and the Divine Spirit; but according to his own words he was perpetually leaving the things that were behind and pressing on to those before, that he might know Christ, and the power of His resurrection, and the fellowship of His sufferings. It is not surprising, therefore, that each of the Epistles contains some profounder apprehension of the fulness and glory of the risen Lord. As Jesus is said to have increased in wisdom and age, so His Apostle was transformed into His image from glory to glory. All his life was a going from strength to strength. And as he climbed the craggy steeps of obedience and faith, of growing likeness to Jesus, of self-sacrifice and experience of the cross, his horizon of knowledge widened to tread the lengths and heights and depths of the knowledge of the love of Christ which still passed his knowledge. We have only to compare the first Epistle to the Thessalonians with that of the Ephesians, to perceive at once how greatly this noble nature had filled out and ripened under the culture of the Divine husbandman.

The best and most natural division of the Epistles, that I have met with, is the following:

The Eschatological Group: 1 and 2 Thessalonians.

The Anti-Judaic Group: 1 and 2 Corinthians, Galatians, Romans.

The Christological, or Anti-Gnostic Group: Philippians, Colossians, Philemon, Ephesians.

The Pastoral Group: 1 Timothy, Titus, and 2 Timothy.

Let us consider them in this order.

1 and 2 Thessalonians

The first of these was probably written towards the close of the year 52, and certainly from Corinth. Timothy had been left in Macedonia to complete the work from which the Apostle had been so summarily torn. After doing all he could to comfort and help the infant churches, he came with Silas to Paul, and the three held solemn and prayerful conferences on the best way of directing and assisting the disciples amid the great storm of opposition through which they were passing. It was impossible for any of them to go to their relief, and so this first Epistle was despatched. And the second from the same city, a few months afterwards, when the Apostle heard that the first had been interpreted to mean that the Lord's coming was near enough to justify the expectation of the speedy dissolution of existing society.

In each of these Epistles, the Apostle dwells more largely than in any of the others on the Second Advent. Its light was illuminating his whole being with its glow. The motive for every duty, the incitement to every Christian disposition, the ground for purity, hopefulness, comfort and practical virtue, are found in the coming of the Son of God. 'The Lord Himself shall descend from heaven with a shout, with the voice of the archangel, and with the trump of God; and the dead in Christ shall rise first; then *we* which are alive and remain shall be caught up.'

The motive for Christian living is less in the sense of the indwelling Christ and more in the expectation of the coming Christ: there is less of the cross, and more of the glory; less of the invisible headship over all things in heaven and earth, which comes out so prominently in later Epistles, and more of the *parousia*, the personal presence of Jesus. To the end the Apostle bade the church stand at her oriel window, looking for the coming of the glory of her great God and Saviour; but the ground covered by his later Epistles is much wider than that of his earliest.

1 Corinthians

Towards the end of Paul's three years' residence in Ephesus, tidings came, partly through Apollos and partly through members of the house of Chloe, of the very unfavourable condition of affairs at Corinth. Amid the strongly sensuous influences of that voluptuous city the little band of converts seemed on the point of yielding to the strong current setting against them, and relapsing into the vices of their contemporaries. Shortly after this a letter arrived from the church itself, brought to Ephesus by Stephanas, Fortunatus and Achaicus, asking advice on a number of practical difficulties. It was a terrible revelation of quarrels, disputings, inconsistencies and grosser evils, and was enough to daunt any man. How could he hope to remedy such a state of things without going in person? And if he went, how would he be received? At that time he was pressed with the terrible conflict which was being waged at Ephesus, and he must stay at his post. There was nothing for it but to write as the Holy Spirit might direct; and the result is the marvellous Epistle, which more than any other has supplied practical direction to the church in the following centuries, showing her how to apply the principles of the gospel to the most complicated moral and social problems. It was carried to Corinth by Titus. In this Epistle there is still the pulse-throb of the Second Advent; but there is, in addition, the sublime conception of the Second Adam, and the revelation by the Holy Spirit now and here, to spiritual minds, of things which eye had not seen, nor ear heard, nor the heart of man conceived.

2 Corinthians

When the riot broke out in Ephesus, the Apostle was eagerly looking for the coming of Titus with tidings of the reception of his Epistle. On his expulsion from the city he went to Troas, making sure that he would meet him there; but failing to do so, he became feverishly anxious, and hastened on to Macedonia to seek him. He was afflicted on every side: 'without were fightings, within were fears', till he was finally comforted by the coming of Titus, who brought good news as he told of their longing, their mourning, their zeal for him. Thereupon he wrote his second

Epistle, and sent it to the church by the hands of Titus and another.

This is the most personal of all his Epistles. He lays bare his heart; he permits us to see its yearning tenderness, its sensitiveness to love or hate, its eager devotion to the best interests of his converts. 'All things are for your sakes... for which cause we faint not.' The deep spiritual aspects of the Christian life, which are so characteristic of the later Epistles, are specially unfolded. He writes as though, under the teaching of the Holy Spirit, he were enjoying increasing measures of the life hid with Christ in God. Though he was always delivered unto death for Jesus' sake, the life of Jesus, which was in him, was manifesting itself in his mortal flesh (4:11). He now knew Christ, not after the flesh, but in the spirit; the constraint of his love was perpetually leading to the denial of self, and the putting on of that new creation which was the gift of the risen Lord (5:14-17). Whatever the difficulties and privations of his lot, he was amply compensated from the eternal and spiritual sphere in which he lived (6:4-10). What though the stake in the flesh cost him continual anguish, the grace of Jesus made him glory in it, as positively a source of strength (12:10).

Galatians
Paul followed Titus to Corinth, and remained there a happy three months. But the joy of fellowship with the large and happy band of friends that gathered around him there must have been greatly blurred by tidings of the fickleness of the Galatians, who were removing 'from him that had called them into the grace of Christ unto another gospel'. Proselytisers had gone amongst his converts professing to represent the church at Jerusalem, and in the name of

185

primitive Christianity had disparaged Paul's apostleship, questioned his authority, and insisted on the necessity of Gentiles being circumcised and submitting to the Levitical law.

It was a critical hour. If these views had prevailed, Christianity must have dwindled into a Jewish sect, and the river of Christian life and work which had gushed from the ground at Pentecost must have lost itself among the sands of Rabbinical speculation. Gentile Christianity was in the balance; the hope of the world at stake. Profoundly stirred in spirit, the Apostle's righteous indignation flames in almost every sentence, and with glowing passion he meets the arguments of those who were seducing the Galatians from the simplicity and freedom of Christ: 'As we said before, so say I now again, if any man preach any other gospel unto you than that ye have received, let him be accursed.'

Under the glow of his indignation there is not only clear and strong thinking, but there is indication of yet further regions of Christian knowledge which were being unfolded to Paul. Pressed by the exigencies of his position - and how often the arising of new heresies has driven God's servants deeper into the fulness treasured in Christ for all needs and times - he is led to realise that not Moses but Abraham, not Sinai but the tents of the patriarch, were the true origin of the Jewish people. Abraham was called when yet in uncircumcision; he believed, and was justified by faith thirty years before he received the distinctive Jewish rite. It was as great a revelation as the shores of the New World to Columbus; and from that moment Paul sprang up to an altogether new position, from which he was able successfully to meet the assaults of the Judaizer, and vindicate all believing Gentiles as children of believing Abraham, and heirs of the covenant of promise.

Romans

As his stay at Corinth drew to a close, the Apostle's mind was attracted to the church in the world's metropolis, which he hoped very soon to visit; and by way of preparation for his coming he prepared a succinct and connected view of the truths which had been revealed to his profoundest thought by the Divine Spirit. Thus originated the greatest of his Epistles, that to the Romans.

In this, as in the former, there is not only a clear appreciation and presentation of the great doctrine of justification by faith, but an ever-enlarging view of our identification with Christ, and of His indwelling. He says we were *reconciled* to God by the *death* of His Son, but we are *saved* by His *life*. He speaks of reigning in life through the abundance of grace treasured up in the one Man, Jesus Christ. His words glow with rapture as he speaks of being joined to Him that was raised from the dead, and of our freedom from the old bondage in which we were held. So entirely had Christ become one with him, and he one with Christ, that he felt the unutterable groans of His intercessions, and something of His travail for the souls of men. He had yielded his members as weapons in his mighty warfare against sin; had been crucified with Christ, and now no longer lived, but Christ lived in him. His life was one of faith in the Son of God, who loved him and gave Himself for him. The cross was the means, not of justification only, but of sanctification, and stood between him and his past; while by the Holy Spirit the Son of God had become resident and regnant within him.

Philippians

There is nothing polemical in this epistle. The former Epistles have met and silenced his detractors and enemies. The strife and divisions of the churches, if such there were, do not reach him through the prison doors, or traverse the distance to his Roman abode. The peace of God that passeth all understanding keeps his mind and heart, and out of that tranquil heart pours forth a tide of deep and tender love to his beloved friends at Philippi.

The hope of being alive at the coming of the Lord is still his heart's guiding-star. His citizenship was in heaven, whence he looked for the Saviour, the Lord Jesus Christ; but the possibility that perhaps the Lord might have to be magnified by his death had already presented itself to his mind. He saw, however, that the will of God was best, and learned from his Master the secret of self-sacrificing humility. Epaphroditus had brought gifts of love from Philippi, and by his hands this letter of love and gratitude was returned.

Colossians

Among those who visited Paul in his hired house, towards the end of his detention in Rome, was Epaphras of Colossae, who also represented Laodicea and Hierapolis - cities of Asia Minor in the valley of the Lycus. He told the Apostle of a strange new heresy, which was developing with alarming rapidity in the churches that had been planted in those distant cities.

The falsely-called Christian philosophy of the time was endeavouring to fill the gulf between sinful man and the holy God by a ladder of mythical existences, through which man's prayers might ascend to God and his blessing descend on man. The whole conception was entirely imaginary, and in its furthest reach must fail of its object; for between the loftiest archangel or spirit and the eternal God there is still the infinite chasm which sunders the creature from the Creator, and is impassable unless the Creator come across it.

The necessity of dealing with this absurd tissue of the imagination was used by the Spirit of God to unveil a wider, deeper view of the fulness that there is in Jesus; and a disclosure was made to the Apostle of the full meaning of the Lord's ascension to the right hand of power. He saw that all principalities and powers, all creature existences, all beings in heaven and earth, and under the earth, were beneath His feet. He was Lord and King, ruling all, filling all, maintaining all. 'In Him were all things created, in the heavens and upon the earth, things visible and things invisible, whether thrones, or dominions, or principalities, or powers, all things have been created through Him, and unto Him: and He is before all things, and in Him all things consist... And ye are complete in Him, who is the head of all principality and power' (Colossians 1:16 RV; 2:10).

At the same time, his conviction of his union with the risen Lord was ever more definite, and his appreciation of His indwelling more full of hope and glory. What did it matter if he was called upon to fill up what was behind of the sufferings? Had it not been given him to make known the riches of the glory of this mystery among the Gentiles, which is Christ in the heart, the hope of glory? Tychicus bore this letter and that to the Ephesians.

Philemon

Onesimus, the runaway slave, fugitive from his master

Philemon, driven by want to the Apostle's house or discovered in some low haunt of crime by his companions in their errands of mercy, had been begotten to a new life, and was now not a slave only, but a brother beloved. Paul sent him back to his master, who was a friend of his, and with whom he seems to have had a business account (verses 18, 19). This Epistle, which is a perfect model of Christian courtesy, was given him as an introduction to his owner.

The chief point to notice here is the perfect patience and certainty with which the Apostle awaits the ultimate triumph of divine love. He must have felt that in the sight of God, Onesimus had a perfect right to freedom; but it would have been highly impolitic for him to interfere between master and man. Let Philemon be taught to look at Onesimus as joined to him in the gospel, it would not be long before he would himself propose his emancipation. But till he did, Paul would not precipitate matters, and Onesimus must return to serve. The principle of action in this single instance doubtless became the ultimate law for the solution of many other difficult problems, which were left to the gradual conquest of the spirit of love.

Ephesians
This Epistle reiterates the great conceptions of the empire of the Lord Jesus, and of His ability to fill the whole gulf between God and man, which the former Epistle (Colossians) had foreshadowed. The doctrine of identification with Christ, in His death, resurrection and ascension, is set forth with remarkable vividness and power. The conception of the church as the Body and Bride of Christ is elaborated with peculiar beauty of detail. But the commanding peculiarity of this Epistle is its allusion to the

home life of husband and wife, parent and child, master and slave.

In earlier days, on account of the present distress, and without the distinct assurance of revelation, the Apostle had spoken as though the difficulties of married life preponderated over its sweets (1 Corinthians 7); but in these later Epistles he holds it up as the model of the love which subsists between the Heavenly Bridegroom and His own; and, contrary to the opinion of his time, he goes so far as to assert that the true bond of marriage is the self-sacrifice of the stronger for the weaker - of the husband for the wife. Woman was no longer to be the slave or toy of man; but men were to be prepared to give themselves for their wives in loving acts of unselfishness, as Christ loved the church and gave Himself for it.

1 Timothy and Titus
After his release, Paul visited the scenes of his former ministry around the shores of the Aegean; and it was during his journeys at this time that he indited these Epistles to direct the young evangelists in the right ordering of the churches under their care. They are of extreme interest because dealing with so many domestic and practical details. He is never weary of showing that the great principles of the gospel are meant to elevate the commoner incidents and duties of life. 'Godliness has promise of the life that now is.' 'The grace of God that bringeth salvation hath appeared unto all men, teaching us that, denying ungodliness and worldly lusts, we should live soberly, righteously, and godly, in this present world' (1 Timothy 4:8; Titus 2:11, 12).

2 Timothy

It was a mellow and softened old age. Lonely so far as dear companions were concerned; full of privations, without cloak, or books, or tendance; shivering in the prison; waiting to be offered, weigh anchor, and drop down the stream. He wanted once more to see his beloved son in the faith, and wrote to speed his steps. It is very pathetic, very beautiful, very human. But the ray of an indomitable courage and faith is flung across the heaving waters: he has kept his Lord's deposit, and knows that the deposit which he had made years before had been no less safely kept. And so the pen is taken in hand for the last time. A few tender messages are added as a postscript. And with large letters he appends the closing sentences, 'The Lord be with thy spirit. Grace be with you.'

The Epistles of Paul resemble stereotyped plates, from which innumerable copies are produced. Who but God can number the myriads of souls that have come in contact with his words, and have themselves become epistles, ministered by him, 'written not with ink, but with the Spirit of the living God'. And, till the Lord come, edition after edition of character, soul-life and blessed victorious experience, shall be struck off from these blocks of holy thinking which we owe to the Apostle Paul.